MONSTERS FROM THE MOVIES

THE WEIRD AND HORRIBLE LIBRARY

Other titles sure to chill and thrill you:

POLTERGEISTS: HAUNTINGS AND THE HAUNTED
by David C. Knight

MUMMIES
by Georgess McHargue

THE WEIRD AND HORRIBLE LIBRARY

MONSTERS FROM THE MOVIES

THOMAS G. AYLESWORTH

J. B. LIPPINCOTT COMPANY

PHILADELPHIA AND NEW YORK

U.S. Library of Congress Cataloging in Publication Data

Aylesworth, Thomas G
  Monsters from the movies.

  (The Weird and horrible library)
  SUMMARY: A survey of the best-known monsters of movies from the
nineteenth century to the present, including discussions of the folklore and
fiction that contributed to their creation and development.
    1. Moving-pictures—Plots, themes, etc.—Horror—Juvenile literature.
[1. Motion pictures—Plots, themes, etc.—Horror] I. Title.
PN1995.9.H6A9   791.43'0909'16   72-1995
ISBN-0-397-31415-9 (pbk.)   ISBN-0-397-31229-6 (lib. bdg.)

*For Stefano Picchi, who knows more about monster movies
than any other fifteen-year-old in Italy
and
for his younger brother, Alessandro, who seems to specialize in
genies.*

CONTENTS

MONSTERS FROM THE MOVIES

CHAPTER 1

COME WITH ME TO THE THEATER

When you come right down to it, the movies are the best medium to use to show the supernatural. We go into the theater; it is dark and spooky, and it is somewhat like being at a séance, waiting for the spiritualist to summon the ghosts of our dear departed. There is darkness, there is concentration, and there is expectancy. There is also a sense of being alone in which one can give way to an image on the screen that is visible but yet not quite believable.

Horror films show us the world we know and recog-

11

nize, but they do it in such a way as to throw us off balance. We know what is waiting for us in the gloomy dark at the top of the stairs, but we are not more confident because we have our hand on the shaky banister.

There are many methods of frightening us. When the camera lingers on a scene for a bit too long, we can become frightened, even though we are only looking at a deserted alley. As a matter of fact, sometimes the anticipation of the fearful happening is more effective than the actual appearance of the thing itself. We are more frightened of the empty, foreboding scene than we are of the scene filled by the specter of a creation of a skillful special effects man.

Now, there are some things that the movies cannot do. For example, there have been very few versions of any merit of stories by two of our most talented horror story writers—Edgar Allan Poe and M. R. James. Both of these writers communicate an almost untranslatable feeling of the supernatural that emerges from our inner feelings, and films cannot do this effectively.

For the most part, Poe's tales are concerned with suffocation, and this means that they include isolation and a great feeling of weight upon our chests. *The Tell-Tale Heart* has a victim beneath the floorboards. *The Cask of Amontillado* tells of a man being walled up alive. *The Black Cat* is about being buried alive. *Berenice* and *A Descent into the Maelstrom* are stories about drowning. How can anyone put this physical feeling on the screen?

The stories of M. R. James usually deal with human

12

There have been attempts to translate Edgar Allan Poe for the screen. Here is a poster for The Black Cat, *released by Universal in 1934.*

13

flesh as it comes in contact with a ghoulish thing. A wallpaper pattern turns to human hair and creeps over the narrator in *The Diary of Mr. Poynter,* or a giant spider drops onto the face of the hero in *The Tractate Middoth,* or a bed sheet with an intense horrible face of linen starts creeping up on the sleeper in *Oh Whistle, and I'll Come to You, My Lad.* The only way that this last could have been put on film was to substitute the sound of the bed sheet for the feel of it. It didn't work.

Of course it is true that horror films on television do not have the same kick that they might have in a darkened theater. *Psycho* and *King Kong* seen on a small screen and in a well-lighted room may not frighten us. But it is true that, if we want to see as many horror films as possible, television is the place where the action is.

The television industry discovered the wonderful world of horror programs early in the game. In the 1950s, Alfred Hitchcock and Boris Karloff were the hosts of two network anthology shows, and once in a while an old film, such as *White Zombie,* could be seen.

Then, in 1957, came "Shock Theater." This program consisted of many of the old Universal horror films that had just been released for television, and a whole new generation could shudder at the original *Frankenstein, Dracula,* and *The Mummy.*

From then on, television viewers were inundated. Rod Serling's "Twilight Zone" was a tremendous success, and is still being seen in reruns. (He has recently repeated his triumph with "Night Gallery.") "Dark Shadows," an

14

afternoon soap opera starring a vampire, was popular for a few years. We were treated to two comedy shows starring monsters—"The Addams Family" and "The Munsters"—both of them in reruns today. And regular weekly showings of horror films, sometimes called "Creature Features" or "Jeepers Creepers," are staples of our television diets.

For those of us who can't get enough horror on the tube, there are horror film festivals at local movie theaters. Even some churches, libraries, and such establishments as YMCAs have shown these films. And there are film clubs and nostalgia clubs that do the same. Some of the best of the monsters are exhibited in night school classes on film making and the history of the movies. Any number of magazines specialize in creepy cinema. There is more than enough exposure of our grisly friends to satisfy all but the most fanatic film buff.

We could almost look upon the typical film of terror as a sort of ladder. On the top rung is the evil one—the monster, the devil, the mad scientist. He is the one with the power.

Next we come to the second rung down. Here we find the normal people—the citizens of Frankenstein's village, the people in the safari who discover King Kong, and so on. These people might be frightened, but they will probably not suffer.

On the third rung there are the people who make up the comic relief—the silly, chattering servants in the castle, the ineffective detectives, the grave diggers. They are put into the picture because they can offer us a few minutes of relaxation between the moments of terror.

Finally, on the bottom rung, we find the real sufferers. These are the hero and heroine, the ones who are cut off from all aid (we think), the helpless maiden and the unarmed youth. Most of the time, they are not as helpless or as unarmed as we expected, but they find their power only in the last reel.

To sum it all up, the ladder is a hierarchy of power. There are vast, indefinable powers at the top and apparent weakness at the bottom. And the confrontation is usually between a single cruel force and one or perhaps two victims.

But what is the strange attraction that these films

A typical scene: the monster and its victim (United Artists Corporation).

have for us? It is probably the immense power that the villains possess. To be sure, we want the bad guy to be conquered in the final scene, but we also want to get several good looks at his evil doings before he exits.

The power that the evil one has is something like a violent thunderstorm, complete with lightning. If you have ever watched a storm and found that you were almost unable to tear your eyes from it, you were experiencing something akin to the power of the horror movie villain.

This power has three characteristics. First of all, it must be mysterious. There is nothing mysterious in the power of a movie gangster with a gun, but Dracula's ability to change normal people into the undead is mysterious.

Next, the power must be tremendous. It must be so strong, as in *Godzilla* or *The Blob,* that it seems unconquerable.

Finally, it must be fascinating. One cannot help but look at it. Take away one or two of these characteristics and you end up with a common, everyday cops-and-robbers film, but add them all up, and you have a horror movie.

The father of the monster movie and the horror film was undoubtedly Georges Méliès. Méliès, born in 1861, was a popular magician and the owner and manager of the Théâtre Robert-Houdin in Paris. The theater was, of course, named after the internationally famous French magician whose name was copied by Erich Weiss of Ap-

17

pleton, Wisconsin, when he took on the stage name of Harry Houdini.

In the beginning, Méliès thought that he might use the movies that had been developed by Edison in America and Louis Lumière in France as a useful addition to, and extension of, his magic acts. He was more interested in optical illusions than he was in making films.

He bought a movie camera and started experimenting. At first he photographed anything that moved. Then came a lucky accident. He was standing in front of the Paris Opéra, taking movies of a bus going along the street. His camera jammed. By the time he had straightened out the trouble, the bus had disappeared, and a hearse was going down the same street. He continued taking his pictures of the hearse. When the film was developed, he had a reel in which a bus turned into a hearse right before the viewers' eyes. Méliès decided to go into the movie business.

In the Parisian suburb of Montreuil he built the world's first film studio. Its walls and ceiling were made of glass in order to let in the light. It had trapdoors in the floor and translucent curtains that were used to get silhouette shots.

Méliès wrote his own scripts, produced his own films, and directed his own actors. Sometimes he himself even appeared in the films. Anyway, we can credit him with being the first motion picture director. People called him "the King of Phantasmagoria," "the Jules Verne of the Cinema," and "the Magician of the Screen."

At the same time, the Lumière brothers were showing films that had more reality—films of trains coming at the audience head-on, etc. The people in the theater would cringe back to get away from the frightening thing coming at them full steam. But while the Lumières were frightening the audiences with motion, Méliès was frightening them with ghostly techniques.

Méliès had happened upon almost all of the tricks that modern cameramen use today. He developed the double exposure to give the impression of ghostly presences. In 1896 he made a woman disappear from the screen by merely stopping the camera and having her step out of range, then starting the camera again—this was the stop-motion photography that was later to be used so successfully in *King Kong*.

He developed a technique of showing underwater scenes by photographing a submerged object through the walls of a fish tank. He discovered fast and slow motion effects and used animation in his films. He discovered how to use the fade, which is the gradual appearance or disappearance of a scene, and the dissolve, which is a slow transition from one image to another image. He experimented continually.

Méliès was the first man in the world to make a film with a real story. It was in 1900, and the story was *Cinderella*. This was the first movie in history that had a story with a beginning, a middle, and an end. He used many of his tricks in it, too. The pumpkin seems actually to turn into a coach; Cinderella's dress, as if by magic, becomes a beautiful gown; and the dancers at the ball are shown in slow motion, as if in a dream.

Méliès was proud of himself. He decided to give up magic and go into the film business completely. He advertised that he was going to make movies involving "transformations, tricks, fairy tales, apotheoses, artistic and fantastic scenes, comic subjects, war pictures, fantasies, and illusions."

His masterpiece was *A Trip to the Moon* in 1902, and the script was borrowed from two sources—Jules Verne's *From Earth to the Moon,* and H. G. Wells's *The First Men in the Moon.* It lasted thirty minutes and told the story, naturally enough, of a trip to the moon. A rocket is fired from a cannon and eventually lands right in the eye of the Man in the Moon, whose face shows a great deal of pain. All sorts of things happen on the moon. An umbrella takes root and starts to grow. Girls in Grecian costumes seem to fly through the air. The astronauts descend into the center of the moon and find beautiful women and gorgeous vegetation. Why they ever come back from this paradise is a mystery.

Then came *The Impossible Voyage,* about a trip to the sun, in 1904, followed by *Tunneling the English Channel* in 1907. Méliès went on to make *The Conquest of the Pole* in 1912. The hero of this picture was the Abominable Giant of the Snows who had the unpleasant habit of eating the members of a polar expedition.

But Méliès was no businessman. Instead of renting out his films to theaters, he sold them outright. His career as

The Abominable Giant of the Snows—Méliès's creation for The Conquest of the Pole, *1912.*

a producer was over in 1914 and he even lost his theater in 1925. Méliès was so upset that he destroyed all of the precious films that he had in his possession and disappeared from sight.

He was not heard of again until 1929, when he was found working as a newsboy in the Paris streets. His friends bought him a little candy stand and he worked there until he was too old and infirm to go on. The father of the movies spent the last days of his life at the old actors' home in Orly and died in 1938, probably never knowing what a debt was owed him by the makers of the modern horror films.

21

CHAPTER 2

MAN-MADE MONSTERS

His yellow skin scarcely covered the work of muscles and arteries beneath; his hair was of a lustrous black, and flowing; his teeth of a pearly whiteness; but these luxuriances only formed a more horrible contrast with his watery eyes, that seemed almost of the same colour as the dun white sockets in which they were set, his shrivelled complexion and straight black lips.

That's the description of Frankenstein's monster that is found in the original book by Mary Shelley, published in 1818. It doesn't sound much like the creature that can be seen in the Frankenstein movies, does it? But this book, written when the author was a girl of nineteen, was probably the first successful fictional account of a man-made monster.

Mary Wollstonecraft Shelley was born in 1797. She married the great English poet Percy Bysshe Shelley in Scotland in 1816, and it was during that year that she began her book.

The Shelleys were on a summer holiday in Switzerland and found that they were neighbors of another famous British poet, George Gordon, or Lord Byron. It seems that it was a miserable summer, rainy and gloomy, and people were staying indoors, amusing themselves as best they could. One of their chief recreations was the reading of ghost stories. Then came an interesting suggestion from Lord Byron. Mrs. Shelley wrote about it:

"We will each write a ghost story," said Lord Byron; and his proposition was acceded to. There were four of us. The noble author began a tale, a fragment of which he printed at the end of his poem of *Mazeppa*. Shelley, more apt to embody ideas and sentiments in the radiance of brilliant imagery, and in the music of the most melodious verse that adorns our language, than to invent the machinery of a story, commenced one founded on the experiences of his early life. Poor Polidori [Dr. John Polidori, a companion of Byron's] had some terrible idea about a skull-headed lady, who was so

23

punished for peeping through a keyhole—what to see I forget—something very shocking and wrong of course; but when she was reduced to a worse condition than the renowned Tom of Coventry, he did not know what to do with her, and was obliged to despatch her to the tomb of the Capulets, the only place for which she was fitted. The illustrious poets also, annoyed by the platitude of prose, speedily relinquished their uncongenial task.

But Mary Shelley did not give up, and her contribution to the festivities was *Frankenstein, or The Modern Prometheus.*

Her *Frankenstein* was not the first description of the search for artificial life. In the third century A.D., an alchemist named Zosimus wrote of a dream that he had had. In the dream was an artificial man—a homunculus. According to Zosimus, a little man appeared in a bottle. He looked as though he were made of copper. Zosimus then changed him into a little silver man, then into a little gold man, helping the transformation along by burning the blood and bones of a dragon. Well, perhaps some people believed him.

At about the same time, the alchemist Simon Magus was accused of taking the spirit from the body of a newly dead boy, putting it into a glass, and changing it first to air, then to water, then to blood, and finally to flesh. Simon Magus thought that it was also possible to change the homunculus back into air.

The first details of how to create a homunculus were revealed by the great physician-alchemist Paracelsus, in the early sixteenth century. He recommended that a man's semen be put in an airtight jar and buried in horse manure for forty days—all the time being held in a magnetic field. During these forty days, a little man will be born in the jar and begin to move. At the end of the period it may look like a man, but it will have one difference— it will be transparent.

The little man must be fed human blood for forty weeks. He also must be kept at a constant temperature, about the same temperature as a mare's womb. After the forty weeks, he will look exactly like a human child, except a great deal smaller.

Paracelsus added a postscript to his formula. "It may be raised and educated like any other child until it grows older and is able to look after itself." That's a far cry from Frankenstein's thunder and lightning formula.

The alchemist Paracelsus, at the age of forty-seven (woodcut by August Hirschvogel).

Even as late as the latter part of the eighteenth century, some scientists were still trying to create a homunculus. While the Minutemen were gathering in Concord and Lexington, a Tyrolean count supposedly manufactured ten little men in ten little bottles.

Another weird man-made monster from out of the past is the golem. This is an artificial man, made of clay or mud, which is brought to life when the name of God is pronounced over it. Some stories say that it is then able to understand orders and is just great for doing housework. Others say that it can be used as a frightening type of bodyguard. But either way it seems that if you have a pet golem, there is trouble right around the corner.

On its forehead is written the Jewish word *emeth,* which means "truth." Every day the golem becomes bigger and bigger, heavier and heavier. Finally it becomes a nuisance, if not a downright danger, to have him around the house. So the first letter of the word on his forehead must be rubbed out. The inscription now reads *meth,* which means "he is dead." The golem will collapse and turn into clay once more.

One story is told of a golem that grew so tall and large that its master could not reach its forehead to rub out the magic letter. So the golem was ordered to take off its shoes. When it bent over to do this, its master quickly erased the first letter. Clever man! Unfortunately the golem turned into a huge lump of clay and fell on top of its master, thereby crushing him to death.

At any rate, the golem deserves a place in man-made

monster literature right along with *Frankenstein.* It has been immortalized in countless folk tales as well as in the book *The Golem,* by Gustav Mayrink, and the play *Der Golem,* by H. Leivick.

But on with the films.

There are probably very few people alive today who have seen the original version of *Frankenstein.* A movie of that name was made in 1910 in the Edison Studios (that's right, Thomas Alva Edison) and all of the prints have since disappeared. In this film, the monster is created in a "cauldron of blazing chemical," according to the press release. That method is closer to the original book than the creation of life by electricity that we are so familiar with in the later productions.

At any rate, this monster was not burned up, drowned, buried in boiling mud, or any other of our favorite ways of creature disposal. He was defeated by the power of love, and he vanished into thin air. Dr. Frankenstein and his lovely wife were free to live happily ever after.

The monster in this film (probably played by Charles Ogle, a member of the Edison Company acting team, although he is given no screen credit) had a pasty face, no neck to speak of, and a wild mane of hair. But the film was not a success because it was too weird for the movie customers of the time.

The second production of *Frankenstein* in our film history was probably the 1915 silent, *Life Without Soul.* In this, the monster was made more human, "awe-inspiring

The EDISON
KINETOGRAM

VOL. 1   LONDON, APRIL 15, 1910   No. 1

SCENE FROM

FRANKENSTEIN

FILM No. 6604

EDISON FILMS TO BE RELEASED
FROM MAY 11 TO 18 INCLUSIVE

MAN-MADE MONSTERS

*The world's first Frankenstein monster, Charles Ogle, on the
cover of a movie magazine.*

but never grotesque." He was played by Percy Darrell
Standing in this production by the Ocean Film Corporation of New York. Apparently the producers did not want
the movie to suffer the same fate as Edison's picture, so
they ended the film with a cop-out that has since become
far too common. It turned out that the whole terrible
thing had merely been a dream of the hero.

Then came the greatest man-made monster film of all
time—the 1931 production of *Frankenstein,* produced by
Carl Laemmle for Universal Studios.

The story of the making of the movie goes like this.
A French film director, Robert Florey, had written a
screenplay based on Mrs. Shelley's book, also borrowing
heavily from the stories of the homunculus and the golem.
The plot was about a scientist who wants to create an
artificial man.

Unfortunately, the scientist's assistant, while he is
picking up spare parts with which to make the body of the
creature, makes a mistake and steals the brain of a dead
criminal. Naturally, when the monster is given life, it cre-
ates all kinds of problems and is eventually killed off by
the angry people who live in a nearby town.

Florey thought that he would be the director of the
film and asked Bela Lugosi, the Hungarian actor, if he
would like to play the monster. The story goes that Lugosi
29

said anyone could play the part under such a heavy load of makeup. Not only that, but it was also rumored that Lugosi was a bit too conceited to want to play a part in which he would not be recognized and would not get a chance to speak.

Meanwhile, James Whale, an English director, saw the screen tests of Lugosi's portrayal, got very interested in the film, and suddenly became the director, replacing Florey. Whale signed Colin Clive, a British actor, to play the good Dr. Frankenstein. But who would play the monster?

There is a story which may or may not be true to the effect that Whale ran into an old acquaintance in the studio commissary—a British actor by the name of William Henry Pratt. Pratt was using the stage and screen name of Boris Karloff.

Whale asked Karloff if he were interested in the role of the monster. Although he didn't think much of the idea of playing a monster, Karloff was a bit too hungry to turn down $125 per week in salary. So Karloff and the great makeup man of Universal Studios, Jack Pierce, worked on the creation of the appearance of the monster.

Pierce turned Karloff into a green-skinned monster. He added struts to the monster's trousers to make Karloff's legs stiff, gave him a steel spine, and had him wear huge boots of the type worn by asphalt spreaders in those days. The makeup took over three hours to put on—every day—and Karloff had to sit through this, put on his forty-eight-pound uniform, go to the set, and act, under a hot

Jack Pierce's triumph—Karloff's makeup.
(Universal, 1931)

August sun shining on southern California. This probably helped him create the role of the suffering monster.

The rest is history, except for the story that Karloff was not even invited to the grand Hollywood opening of the picture. It wasn't that the studio bosses were being cruel to him. It was merely part of a big publicity stunt. The name of the actor who played the monster was not revealed until the picture was released. This was supposed to make the public curious enough to come to the theaters in droves—which it did.

A couple of scenes were cut from the original version of the film before it was seen by the public. One of them shows the monster roaming through the countryside. He comes upon a little girl who is throwing flowers into a stream. The girl is too young to be afraid of the monster, and he, obviously seeking human affection, sits down beside her and joins in her game. But he cannot tell the difference between a flower and human life. At this point comes the cut made by the studio in the prints shown in the United States. Without knowing that he is doing anything wrong, the monster throws the girl into the stream and she drowns.

The other cut scene was taken out by the British censor. The prints of the film shown in England do not contain the scene in which the monster, after being constantly taunted by Dr. Frankenstein's cruel assistant, turns on him and hangs him.

Because of the macabre nature of the settings, it is probably a good thing that *Frankenstein* was shot in black and white, rather than color (color was available at that time). A color print would have destroyed some of the eerie atmosphere. But a few prints were made of the film using a green tint over the whole screen, and it is said that this coloring made the production even more horrifying. Green is the symbolic color for horror, anyway, and the tint seemed to make the lips and the shadows on the face of the monster turn black—the better to frighten us.

One of the most important things to be found in this picture is the idea, unusual for the time, that a horror film must be basically logical, that every strange event must have some sort of a rational explanation. Take the makeup used by Boris Karloff as the monster. He has a square skull —the result of the basic cut used on cadavers in primitive dissections. He has electrodes on his neck to be hooked up to wires that carry the electric life force.

The logic in *Frankenstein* worked beautifully, but many films of today suffer because of the imagined need for rational explanations. We seldom see a film that requires us really to believe in monsters, ghosts, or other supernatural beings. These horrors are usually explained away as being the products of man's mind. Ghosts turn out to be curtains blowing in the wind, magicians turn out to be tricksters, and haunted houses turn out to be figments of the imaginations of terrified heroines.

But in *Frankenstein,* the director, James Whale, was able to concoct an atmosphere of real sin, in the sense of a crime against a Divine Being. Dr. Frankenstein, the film tells us, was really trying to usurp God's power. Add to that the great acting job turned in by Karloff—a portrayal, not of a horrible, cruel beast, rather a martyr who didn't ask for life, but who was a product of another's sin—and we begin to realize just how great this movie was.

By the way, in the book the good doctor's first name was Victor, and why Hollywood decided to change it to Henry is anybody's guess. Also, who knows why they never gave the monster a name in the movie? Perhaps it was the fact that he had no name in the picture that caused whole generations of moviegoers to call the monster "Frankenstein" and forget that that was the scientist's name. The film fan didn't know what else to call the ugly creature. In the book he was called Adam, and this underlines the idea of a sin against God. Frankenstein had had the gall to name his creature after the first man in the Bible.

Hollywood learned a lesson from *Frankenstein.* Monsters can be profitable. The film had cost a mere seven hundred fifty thousand dollars to make, and, to date, has earned more than thirteen million dollars. With profits like this, who would blame the movie makers for bringing out more and more pictures starring the monster of Frankenstein?

The first sequel was quite good. In fact, some film critics have said that it was better than the original. Whale and Karloff, along with Colin Clive, had struck again with *The Bride of Frankenstein* in 1935.

In this movie, as was the case in the book, the monster wants companionship. So it's back to the laboratory for the good doctor. At the end of the film, he has created an artificial female (played by Elsa Lanchester) who takes one look at her intended husband and will have nothing to do with him.

One of the most touching examples of the innate humanity of the monster occurs at this point. While his lady is screaming in horror, he reaches out to pat her hand, trying to show her that he needs somebody to love. This doesn't work, however, and, shedding a tear, he directs the doctor and his wife to leave the laboratory. After

Frankenstein did it again! A scene from The Bride of Franken-stein *(Universal, 1935). From left to right: Colin Clive, Elsa Lanchester, Boris Karloff, Ernest Thesiger.*

they leave, he blows up the lady monster and, incidentally, himself along with her.

The makeup designed for Elsa Lanchester was based upon the famous ancient representation of the head of the Egyptian queen Nefertiti. By the way, in this film, Dr. Frankenstein's scientist friend, Dr. Pretorius (played by Ernest Thesiger), has been playing around with the creation of homunculi. He keeps them in bottles and dresses them as dancers, kings, etc.

In 1939, along came *The Son of Frankenstein.* In this film, Basil Rathbone played Wolfgang Frankenstein and attempted to carry on the family tradition of making the monster come back to life. It really wasn't a bad film, although it was nowhere near as well done as the first two had been.

One area of production in *The Son of Frankenstein* deserves comment, however. In the first two American films, the settings of the rooms of the castle were spooky enough. But in this sequel, the viewer really gets the horror treatment. Frankenstein's son is traveling back to his father's castle on a train. He looks out of the windows and sees the countryside gradually changing from a happy, bright landscape to one that is slowly becoming bare and misty—just the right type of country for creating a monster. Indeed, Basil Rathbone is entering a new world, and the people in the theater are going right along with him.

Of course, Karloff played the monster in the production, and another master of screen horror joined him. It was our old friend, Bela Lugosi. In *The Son of Franken-stein,* he played the monster's loyal friend, Igor, a mad shepherd who had a hideously broken neck. It seems that he had been the victim of an unsuccessful hanging.

After the first three Frankenstein films in which Karloff appeared, the monster seemed to go downhill. In 1942 came *The Ghost of Frankenstein,* without the great Karloff, who had apparently had enough.

In this film, lo and behold, the movie makers had found out that the original Dr. Frankenstein had had another son! In addition to Wolfgang, who had washed his hands of the monster-making business, Henry had fathered Ludwig (played by Sir Cedric Hardwicke).

But who would play the monster now? The studio picked Lon Chaney, Jr., son of the famous horror man of the silent screen. Picking up Igor, the misshapen shepherd of *The Son of Frankenstein* (again played by Lugosi), he slogged onto the screen in those eighteen-pound boots.

Beginning with *The Ghost of Frankenstein,* the monster was a mere shadow of his former self. He lost his powers of communication, limited though they were, as well as his ability to make us feel sympathetic toward the artificial creature who does not understand the rules of the game of life.

We can't blame all of this on Chaney's acting, either. He had already been successful playing the character Lawrence Talbot in the Wolf Man film, and later in his career he was to give really remarkable performances in such films as *High Noon.* We must also blame the script writers. They were beginning to make a parody out of Frankenstein films. In *The Ghost of Frankenstein* we have a scientist who is even more careless than his father and brother before him. He hopes to reform the monster by removing his brain and putting in a better model. But whose brain does he mistakenly use? That's right—Igor's. Who could turn in a convincing performance in a film with a plot like that?

The next entry came the following year, 1943. Somebody decided that the monster needed some help, so out came *Frankenstein Meets the Wolf Man.* When Universal cast the picture, they realized that Chaney must go back to his werewolf role which had been a great success two years before in *The Wolf Man.* Finally, after twelve years, Bela Lugosi got another chance to play the monster. He wasn't as good as Karloff (nobody could have been), and his makeup left something to be desired. But he was playing the part of a monster that had been blinded in *The Ghost of Frankenstein,* and naturally he was clumsy.

In 1944 there was *The House of Frankenstein,* a sort of monster party of the day. If, as in *Frankenstein Meets the Wolf Man,* two monsters appealed to movie audiences, how about making a film with three monsters? So they added Dracula, the other major movie monster of the era. Chaney stayed in as the Wolf Man, John Carradine played Dracula, and the studio picked Glenn Strange to play the Frankenstein monster. Strange had previously been most famous for playing the bad guy in cowboy movies.

In 1948, the monster, who had met his Maker in every previous film, met something else again—Abbott and Costello. In *Abbott and Costello Meet Frankenstein,* there is an attempt to put the brain of Lou Costello into the head of the monster. Obviously, the Frankenstein picture series had hit rock bottom.

Or had it? In 1957, *I Was a Teenage Frankenstein* was released. The monster in this was created out of parts of teen-agers. And the film even made the basic mistake that generations of moviegoers had been making. Frankenstein in this film was the monster, not the doctor.

In the 1950s, the British began to take over. Hammer Studios released *The Curse of Frankenstein* in 1957. It starred Peter Cushing as Frankenstein and Christopher Lee as the monster. Lee's makeup was quite different from Karloff's, since Universal still owned the copyright for the original. In *The Curse of Frankenstein,* Lee looked as though he had been created out of scar tissue and greasepaint.

With this film, a new day had dawned. Hammer spent little time in developing characterizations, sympathy, or even suspense. The film seemed to concentrate on blood and guts, with a little sex thrown in. Three different versions of this film were shot and released in different countries—a mild one, with a few shocking scenes; a medium one, with a few extra buckets of blood; and a no-holds-barred zinger with the blood flowing like wine.

Hammer followed *The Curse of Frankenstein* with *The Revenge of Frankenstein* in 1958, and the dam had

Christopher Lee, the British counterpart to Boris Karloff, in
The Curse of Frankenstein *(Hammer, 1957).*

MAN-MADE MONSTERS

burst. That same year gave us *Frankenstein 1970* (an American film starring Boris Karloff, not as the monster, but as the doctor) and *Frankenstein's Daughter* (a British film from Astor Studios). And in the following years, there were produced:

> *El Infierno del Frankenstein* (Mexico), 1963
> *El Testamento del Frankenstein* (Mexico), 1964
> *The Evil of Frankenstein* (Britain, Hammer), 1964
> *Frankenstein Conquers the World* (Japan), 1965
> *Frankenstein Meets the Space Monster* (U.S.), 1965
> *Jesse James Meets Frankenstein's Daughter* (U.S.), 1965
> *Frankenstein Created Woman* (Britain, Hammer), 1967
> *Frankenstein Must Be Destroyed* (Britain, Hammer), 1969

But not since the 1931 film have Frankenstein and his friend really been treated properly. They have been laughed at, made to look like madmen, and even turned into cartoon characters.

As far as the golem is concerned, the first film about him was a German picture, *Der Golem,* made in 1915. The picture was directed by Paul Wegener, who also played the title role. It was the story of the discovery of a clay statue which is then sold to an antique dealer. The merchant brings it to life. But the golem falls in love with

41

the dealer's daughter, and when he realizes that she is terrified of him, he tries to destroy the city. The golem is stopped only by a terrible fall from a high tower.

The golem in this film was a creature who had many human qualities. It seems certain that this movie was a forerunner of the 1931 *Frankenstein,* with its emotional monster.

Der Golem was, unfortunately, released in the United States (and retitled *The Monster of Fate)* during the week in which diplomatic relations were broken off with Germany prior to World War I. Needless to say, the public did not react favorably to this German import.

In 1920, Wegener came back with a better version of the tale, also titled *Der Golem.* French movie makers got into the act in 1936 with *Le Golem,* and remade it, using the same title, in 1966.

But the golem went the way of Frankenstein's monster. In 1917 appeared a German film (directed by Wegener) called *Der Golem und die Tänzerin (The Golem and the Dancer)* that must have been as embarrassing as *Abbott and Costello Meet Frankenstein.* And there was a Czechoslovakian film of 1951 called *The Emperor and the Golem.*

The golem turned up in London in 1966 in a film entitled *It.* Roddy McDowall plays a museum employee who discovers a golem in a warehouse. He orders it to kill his employer and kidnap his girl friend. Poor Roddy is killed by a bomb, and the golem disappears in the ocean. He may be back.

It wasn't for lack of advertising that Der Golem *was a flop in the United States—a commercial message from* The Moving Picture World, *March 31, 1917.*

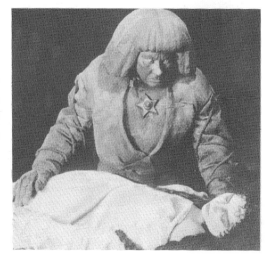

In the remake of Der Golem, *Paul Wegener gazes at his beloved, Lyda Salmonova (UFA, 1920).*

A partial man-made monster was created in 1925, in an Austrian film, *Orlacs Haende.* In this goody, a concert pianist loses his hand and a strange scientist gives him a new one. But the new one is really the hand of a murderer. You can guess the rest—the hand takes over the brain of the good guy, turning him into a bad guy. This film was remade in 1961 and released in the United States under the title of *The Hands of Orlac,* with such celebrated actors as Mel Ferrer and Christopher Lee.

There was actually a movie titled *Homunculus,* made in Germany in 1916. It was one of the early serials, consisting of six hour-long episodes, and was about a creature without a soul who had been created by a mad scientist. This may sound familiar, but the monster falls in love with

44

a beautiful girl, finds out that the girl hates him, and decides to try to wreck the world. Eventually, at the end of
the sixth hour of the film, the homunculus is struck dead
by lightning. The horror of this monster seems not to have
been great enough for any studio to be tempted into making a sequel.

So, the last man-made monster lies in his grave. This
seems a fitting point to end the chapter—before they all
come back in *Frankenstein and the Golem Meet the
Hand of the Homunculus.*

CHAPTER 3

SELF-MADE MONSTERS

. . . Late one accursed night, I compounded the elements, watched them boil and smoke together in the glass, and when the ebullition had subsided, with a strong glow of courage, drank off the potion. The most racking pangs succeeded; a grinding in the bones, deadly nausea, and a horror of the spirit. . . . Then these agonies began swiftly to subside, and . . . I felt younger, lighter, happier in body. . . . I knew myself to be wicked. . . .

That's what happens when you change yourself from kindly Dr. Jekyll, true friend and family physician, to evil

Edward Hyde, hellrake, murderer, and candidate for Mr. Ugly. In *The Strange Case of Dr. Jekyll and Mr. Hyde,* written in 1886 by Robert Louis Stevenson, Henry described his new body: "Edward Hyde was so much smaller, slighter, and younger than Henry Jekyll. . . . Evil was written broadly and plainly on the face. . . . Evil . . . had left on that body an imprint of deformity and decay. . . . Edward Hyde, alone in the ranks of mankind, was pure evil."

Well, he brought it on himself.

The self-made monster is one of the most popular of all of the basic horror themes in film. Sometimes it is a mad scientist who experiments upon himself, as Dr. Jekyll did, and sometimes it is a stupid, but innocent, man who does something dumb, such as selling his soul to the devil or making himself into a werewolf. But the result is the same. Our hero is to blame.

Let's take that good old pact with the devil. It is based upon the ancient belief that the Prince of Darkness is greedy for human souls and anyone is fair game. Usually the devil promises to reward the poor unfortunate somehow in exchange for the victim's soul after death.

There are many stories of these pacts, and, oddly enough, quite a few of them describe the defeat of the devil. For example, there was young Proterius, who was supposed to have lived in the fourth century A.D. He signed a paper for the devil, renouncing his Christian beliefs, and the devil helped him out by causing Proterius's master's daughter to fall in love with the young man.

St. Basil saved Proterius by forcing the devil to give back the paper.

Theophilus of Adana, in the sixth century A.D., pulled the same stunt. But he, it is said, got help straight from the Virgin Mary. And one of the legends about Roger Bacon, the thirteenth-century philosopher and alchemist, says that he promised the devil to join him in hell if he (Bacon) died neither in a church nor out of it. Would you believe that Bacon then built himself a room in the wall of a church and carefully arranged to die there—neither inside nor out?

But the most famous pact-signer was Faust, the legendary philosopher. Depending upon whose version of the story you read, he either beat the devil or he didn't. One group of writers gets him off the hook, after a life of youth and love, while another group has a more startling story to tell. They say that Faust was urged to break his promise, but he said, "The devil has honestly kept the promise that he made to me, therefore I will honestly keep the pledge that I made and contracted with him."

About midnight on Faust's last day on earth, it is said, there came a storm, accompanied by sounds of hissing and whistling as though from thousands of snakes. When the neighbors came out of their houses the next morning, all that remained of Faust was a pitiful pile of flesh in the yard. Inside his study, however, they found blood all over the place, brains and teeth on the floor, and his eyeballs pinned to the wall.

It shouldn't come as any surprise to learn that man,

Faust, at right, being tempted by Mephistopheles (from Umrisse zu Goethe's Faust, *by Moritz Retzsch, 1834). The theme of a pact with the devil was part of literature long before the birth of movies.*

since the dawn of time, has been nervous around wolves. Probably cavemen used to huddle in their caves, listening to the far-off cries of these beasts. What could be more natural than to dream up stories in which men turned themselves into wolves and wandered all around the countryside looking for fresh meat?

It may have started in Greece with the old legend of Lycaeon (from whose name our modern word meaning "werewolfism"—lycanthropy—comes), who was changed into a wolf by the chief god of Greece, Zeus. There are werewolf stories from almost every country in which the animal was found. And in those countries where there are few or no wolves, there are other werebeasts to take their

49

place. Eskimos have their werewhales, South American Indians have their werejaguars, and so on.

One point should be made here. With the exception of a few stories, such as that one about Lycaeon, the legend is that the werewolf brings his strange state upon himself. Most wolf-man films credit the hero's change into a beast to the bite of another werewolf. This is probably a case of confusing werewolves with vampires.

One ancient Greek writer told of a man who took off all of his clothing, swam in an enchanted pool, and was thus turned into a wolf. By the way, he could change back into a man by refusing meat for nine years and then swimming in the same pool, but that's a long time to wait and the wolf was liable to get very hungry.

There were supposed to be other means of transformation, of course. Sleep on the ground in an open field on a Friday night when the moon is full, for example. In the

An eighteenth-century drawing of "The Wild Beast of Gévaudan"— allegedly a French werewolf active in 1764 and 1765.

50

Balkan states (where Transylvania is located), a mysterious flower, when eaten, could do the job. Or you can drink water from a wolf's footprint, or from a stream where wolves have quenched their thirst. On the other hand, perhaps you would prefer to eat the brain of a wolf.

One of the surefire ways went something like this. Wait for a full moon, then go up to the top of a hill and let the moon shine down upon you. When the clock strikes twelve midnight, draw a magic circle around yourself on the ground. This circle must be three feet in diameter. Then draw another circle, seven feet in diameter, around the first circle, and you are almost ready to begin.

Start a fire under a cauldron in the middle of the inner circle, and pour in a variety of herbs, spices, soot, fat from young babies, and other repulsive materials. Then there is a special verse to recite. Smear your body with the gunk from the pot and drape a wolf's skin over your body. And wait. And wait. Eventually, you are supposed to become a werewolf.

One nice thing about these beliefs is that (again, unlike the wolf-man movies) it is alleged to be possible to turn back permanently into a man. Not that it's easy. Perhaps you merely go through the rigamarole backwards. Or you can have a friend draw three drops of blood from your body and hit you on the head three times with a knife. The surest method, it seems, was to kneel down on the ground in the same spot for a period of one hundred years.

And there are ways to avoid having to put up with

werewolves. Stay near running water, or keep some rye, mistletoe, or ash or yew branches handy. These beasts are mortally afraid of streams and certain vegetables, it is said.

Let's go to the movies. Probably the most popular characters in the self-made monster films are Dr. Jekyll and Mr. Hyde. In the Stevenson story, Dr. Jekyll is a loveable character and represents the urge to do good that is present in all men's minds. Mr. Hyde, on the other hand, represents the evil that is also present in all of us.

Jekyll has discovered a potion that will turn him into Hyde, and he drinks the stuff. Fortunately, he also had found another concoction that would turn Hyde back into Jekyll. This goes on for a time, back and forth, back and forth, until Dr. Jekyll finds out that, in the form of Mr. Hyde, he has committed a murder. At that point he decides to try to kick the habit.

The problem now is that he finds that he is turning into Hyde without taking the potion. So soon he has to take double doses of the antidote in order to turn back into Dr. Jekyll. The final blow comes when he runs out of one of the ingredients in the brew and finds himself unable to change back again into his former sweet self. So he commits suicide.

Probably the primary reason for the popularity of the Jekyll and Hyde films—and the story was filmed over and over—was that, in the early days of the movies, motion pictures were thought of as being evil influences on the minds of the people in the audience, and were often denounced from pulpits all over the land. So what could be more natural than to film a story in which there was such a clear separation between good and evil? Dr. Jekyll is all good, and Mr. Hyde is all bad. And add to all this the fact that, in the end, good was able to eliminate evil.

The 1908 production of *Dr. Jekyll and Mr. Hyde,* made by Selig Polyscope in the United States, was a pretty primitive film. The producers gathered a company of actors who were touring in a play based upon the Stevenson novelette, let them act on a Chicago stage, and filmed their actions. Each scene in the movie even opened with a rising curtain.

The next version of the tale was *Den Skaebnesvangre Opfindelse,* released in the United States as, of course, *Dr. Jekyll and Mr. Hyde.* This was made by a Danish film company named Nordisk (the Great Northern Company) in 1910.

In 1912, Thanhouser Studios came out with another American version, *Dr. Jekyll and Mr. Hyde,* starring James Cruze, who later went on to become a successful director; Harry Benham; and Marguerite Snow, Cruze's wife. The unusual thing about this version is that, for the only time in history, two actors were used for the two title roles.

The director of this film was Lucius Henderson, who decided to shoot the whole thing from a fixed camera position with no changes in lighting. Mercifully, his picture was a one-reeler and so was over before the audience could get up the courage to demand its money back.

The year of 1913 gave us a bumper crop of films about

the strange duo. There was the German picture called *Der Anderer* and a British movie, *Dr. Jekyll and Mr. Hyde,* shot in a primitive color process called Kineto-Kinemacolor. An American version was made by Universal Studios that same year. It starred King Baggott and Jane Gail. One of the reasons that this was not too much of a success was probably the fact that the dual roles of Jekyll and Hyde require a master actor. And King Baggott was not in the same league as some later Jekyll-Hydes— John Barrymore, Fredric March, and Spencer Tracy.

There are those who believe that the first important terror film to be made following World War I was the 1920 *Dr. Jekyll and Mr. Hyde,* produced by Famous Players. The title roles were played by the gifted actor John Barrymore. The director, John Stuart Robinson, adapted the Stevenson story for the screen and introduced an ele-

John Barrymore, as the unpleasant Mr. Hyde, talking with Louis Wolheim, in Dr. Jekyll and Mr. Hyde *(Paramount, 1920).*

ment of sex to the screenplay. Where the original Hyde of the novelette was a mere animalistic killer, in this film he became a sadistic sex murderer.

In the film, Dr. Jekyll is a virginal young gentleman in Victorian England who is coaxed by his friends into going to a stag party. Here his sexual interest is aroused and, naturally, so is the same instinct in Mr. Hyde.

Barrymore, at the time, was one of the top actors in the film world. And he milked the transformation scene for all that he could get out of it. The camera focuses on Dr. Jekyll, full face. Slowly he raises the evil brew to his lips and drinks. His body stiffens, his face assumes a look of pain. Then he falls from his chair to the floor (out of range of the camera). The camera at this point was stopped while the actor donned his ugly makeup, then shooting started again. When the actor gets up—behold! —he is Mr. Hyde.

John Barrymore was great. In the film, made on Long Island in the Paramount Studios, he became a handsome, dashing Jekyll and a horrifying fanged, taloned Hyde. He was able to appeal to his feminine admirers as Jekyll and perform some fantastic emoting as Hyde—altogether an ideal setup for him.

This picture was so successful that a rival producer, Louis B. Mayer, made a quickie version that same year. It starred Sheldon Lewis, but it was a cheap imitation that had the additional drawback of including the old cop-out again—Dr. Jekyll awakes and finds that the whole thing was a dream.

Almost lost in the 1920 Jekyll and Hyde shuffle was a German picture, *Der Januskopf.* This starred the fine actor, Conrad Veidt, and was the last of the silent films on the subject.

Fredric March was the next Jekyll and Hyde in the 1932 film directed by Rouben Mamoulian. And March was the first actor (and the only one to date) to win an Academy Award for appearing in a monster film. This *Dr. Jekyll and Mr. Hyde* was the first sound movie based upon the Stevenson story. Aside from a top-notch performance

A before-and-after picture of Fredric March as Dr. Jekyll and Mr. Hyde *(Paramount, 1932).*

56

by March, the most outstanding thing about the picture was that the camera looked Jekyll right in the face all during his transformation into Hyde. And without the help of a photographic laboratory.

Mamoulian never explained how he was able to pull this off. But there are those who say that he used infrared film, subtle changes in lighting, and special makeup that is visible in some types of lighting and not in others.

March gave a great performance in this movie. There was a similarity between his interpretation and the interpretation of the monster role that Karloff had given in *Frankenstein.* Both Hyde and the monster were primitive men looking for pagan fulfillment. March's Hyde drinks the pouring rain gleefully in the same way Karloff's monster stood in awe of the first sunbeam that he saw.

Add to all of this an assortment of weird sound effects, including a beating heart, and the film came out as a landmark version of the old story. Indeed, in spite of the fact that the 1941 edition starred Spencer Tracy, Ingrid Bergman, and Lana Turner, March's film was the better of the two.

This is not to say that Tracy was bad as the heroes of *Dr. Jekyll and Mr. Hyde.* Actually he was quite good. He used a minimum of makeup—mostly fake eyebrows and eye shadow—and let his own talent supply the rest of the personality of Hyde. But the script was dreary and the director (Victor Fleming, coming fresh from his triumphant direction of *Gone with the Wind)* went in for a lot of dream sequences that tended to slow down the action.

That was the last of the straight Jekyll and Hyde films. Hollywood, used to bringing monsters back to life, decided to try the same thing with Mr. Hyde. So it was decided to drum up the offspring of Dr. Jekyll, even though he lived and died a bachelor in the Stevenson tale.

So we had Louis Hayward starring as the *Son of Dr. Jekyll* in 1951. And there was another sibling appearing as the *Daughter of Dr. Jekyll* in 1957. The cute thing about this film is that the daughter did not turn out to be the monster. Rather, it was her guardian, an old friend of Dr. Jekyll, who turned into a fiend from time to time.

Even Boris Karloff once got into the act. He played Mr. Hyde in the 1953 film *Abbott and Costello Meet Dr. Jekyll and Mr. Hyde*. While it did nothing for his career, it undoubtedly kept the paychecks rolling in.

Then Hammer Studios in England could not resist a remake of something approaching a Jekyll and Hyde film in 1960. Loaded with sex, this movie told the story of a certain Dr. Jekyll who is married to a cheating wife. In the form of Hyde, he tries to make love to his own wife. From that point on, the story gets further and further away from Stevenson and the result, called *House of Fright* in the United States and *The Two Faces of Dr. Jekyll* in Britain, was a box office bomb.

A French version, *The Testament of Dr. Cordelier,* was released in the United States under the title of *Experiment in Evil* in 1961. It was directed by the great Jean Renoir and starred the fine actor Jean-Louis Barrault. In this film, based upon the Stevenson tale, M. Opale (Hyde) is part killer, part clown character, and more of an anarchist than a beast.

Oh, there have been other versions of the story. There was *Il Dottore Jekyll* (Italian, 1951), and there was *Il Mio Amico Jekyll* (also Italian, 1960). But the end of the line, for the time being, of the Jekyll and Hyde story may be the 1963 Jerry Lewis film, *The Nutty Professor.* This is a caricature of the original, featuring the dull, clumsy Professor Kelp and the irresistible Mr. Love, both played by Lewis.

One of the earliest films about a pact with the devil was *The Student of Prague,* made in 1913, starring our old golem friend, Paul Wegener. Here we have a poor student named Baldwin who signs up with a representative of the devil, the wizard Scapinelli. He is rewarded with the girl of his dreams and trades this for all rights to his image in the mirror. Baldwin beats the girl's boyfriend in a duel by the use of magic. But this angers the girl's family and Baldwin loses out to the devil. The film was so successful that it was remade, as was *The Golem,* after World War I.

Perhaps the greatest satanic pact movie of all time was *The Picture of Dorian Gray,* taken from the short novel of the same name written by Oscar Wilde in 1891. Young handsome Dorian (played by Hurd Hatfield) is having his portrait painted. Dorian admires his youth and beauty in the painting and wishes that he might be forever as handsome as he is in the picture. Now the plot thickens.

The years go on and Gray remains forever young. He leads the most evil life, yet not a wrinkle appears on his face. But after each crime, each vicious act, that he commits, the portrait changes, gradually becoming a thing of horror. Finally, Dorian can no longer stand to look at the painting, and hacks away at it with a knife. But he has destroyed his own soul, and he falls dead before the portrait. When his friends find his body, it is lying in front of the painting. And the painting appears as it was in the beginning, but his remains on the floor are "withered, wrinkled and loathsome of visage. It was not until they had examined the rings that they recognized who it was."

This story was the basis for a few minor film scripts during the silent days, under other titles. But not until the Hurd Hatfield, George Sanders, Angela Lansbury production of 1945 was it a success. Much of this acclaim was due to the magnificent paintings, by the Albright brothers, of poor Dorian Gray withering away.

The first werewolf picture, called, naturally enough, *The Werewolf,* was made in the United States in 1913. But actually it was a wolf *girl* film and was based upon an old Navajo legend. Watuma, an Indian girl, comes back to life one hundred years after her death to look for the ghost of the evil man who had killed her boyfriend. To accomplish this, she, for some reason or other, decides to turn herself into a wolf.

The wolf *man* did not arrive on the scene until 1935. One of the reasons for this long delay was probably that there was no piece of fiction to tie the script to as was the case with *Frankenstein, Dracula,* and *Dr. Jekyll and Mr. Hyde.* At any rate, in that year *The Werewolf of London* made his appearance.

The werewolf of London is really an eccentric botanist who is attacked by a real werewolf while on an expedition. The purpose of this trip is to discover a rare plant called the *Marifasa lupina,* which blooms only in the moonlight.

The botanist brings the plant back to London and proceeds to wait for it to bloom. Then a Japanese scientist appears, asking for the *Marifasa.* It turns out that this Japanese scientist is really the werewolf who attacked the botanist. He wants the plant because it cures the dreaded disease of lycanthropy, but it turns out that the botanist is a werewolf, too. The Japanese gets away with the plant, and the loveable botanist is killed by a silver bullet.

Henry Hull in his makeup for The Werewolf of London *(Universal, 1935).*

This film, from Universal Studios, starred Henry Hull. But it was not the best of all werewolf pictures, since it was really a takeoff from the Jekyll and Hyde films. Here we have a kindly physician who is bitten by a werewolf and keeps being transformed into a savage beast. When they counted up their money, the studio owners found out that this picture was not quite a financial success.

But then, in 1941, the studio decided to try again, and hired writer Curt Siodmak to create another lycanthrope for them. The result was *The Wolf Man.*

Jack Pierce, of *Frankenstein* fame, was the makeup man responsible for the horrible appearance of the wolf man, who was played by Lon Chaney, Jr. It is said that it took five hours per day to apply the makeup, and when the changes took place on camera, it really became complicated. As the hero changes into the wolf man, yak hairs (that's right, yak hairs) were glued to his face, in little clumps. Then the film was exposed, a few frames at a time; more hairs were added, more film exposed, until the whole hairy face and the furry hands were visible.

The Wolf Man is the story of Lawrence Talbot, a happy college student, who goes back to the home of his ancestors somewhere in Transylvania. Transylvania is the ancient home of horror. Bram Stoker may have started this idea when he imagined that Castle Dracula could be found there. Or perhaps it was the superstitious peasants who lived there. They were influenced by the large Gypsy population, and picked up Gypsy tales of werewolves and vampires. At any rate, Transylvania is the logical home of

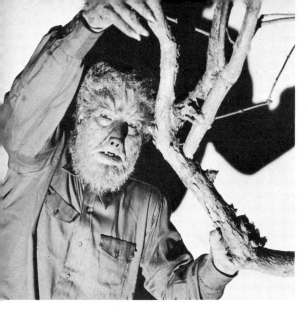

Jack Pierce strikes again! Here is his makeup on Lon Chaney, Jr. as The Wolf Man *(Universal, 1941).*

the mad scientist and the monster. It is an area with dark mountains, swamps, gloomy forests, and lots of fog—just the place for a story of horror.

Here, in approximately the same region made famous in the Frankenstein films, Talbot goes out for a moonlight stroll. He breaks up a fight between a werewolf and a beautiful young girl, only to be bitten in the process. He then becomes a werewolf himself.

Let us point out again that the werewolves of legend were more interested in tearing their prey to bits and eating them than they were in merely biting them. So, to be bitten by a werewolf was just the first step—it was usually impossible to survive in order to become a werewolf yourself.

At any rate, Talbot starts having what he thinks are

dreams. He thinks that he has killed people and consults an old Gypsy woman. She tells him that her own son, who is a werewolf, was the one who turned Talbot into a werewolf. The proof is a pentagram that appears in the palm of his hand. Her other wonderful news is that he can only return to normal by means of a silver bullet or some other silver object, and then he will have a chance to be normally dead. That's not really returning to normal, is it?

Talbot picks his victims when he sees a reproduction of the mysterious pentagram in the palms of their hands. The pentagrams that Talbot sees are illusions, of course, and are merely indications of who the next victim will be. Naturally, he begins to dread the coming of the full moon, during which time he will become a wolf. Finally, he is killed by his own father, who clubs him to death with his silver-headed cane.

This picture about the twenty-six-year-old college boy was an instant success when it was released. And part of the credit for the success goes to two other masters of horror—Bela Lugosi as the son of the gypsy, and Claude Rains as the senior Talbot.

Our poor friend Lawrence Talbot was brought back again and again. In *Frankenstein Meets the Wolf Man,* made in 1943, and previously mentioned, he fought with the monster, played not too well by Bela Lugosi. Actually, Chaney did not fare too well in these pictures, either. With all that makeup on, about the only acting that he was permitted to do was to stare agonizingly up at the full moon—waiting for nature to take its course.

In this film, Talbot brings the monster back to life, only to have (in his wolf suit) a fight with him in the final reel. At the end of the fight, both monsters supposedly drown. But they are not dead, of course.

In the next film, *The House of Frankenstein* (1944), the monster returns the favor and brings the wolf man back to life. This time our furry friend is killed by a silver bullet, but he returns again in 1945 in *The House of Dracula.* In this picture he is alleged to have been cured of lycanthropy, but it doesn't last for long. And we can't forget the bottom of the barrel—*Abbott and Costello Meet Frankenstein* (1948), in which the wolf man saves Lou Costello from an evil doctor who wants to put Costello's brain in Frankenstein's monster, grabs Dracula, and leaps into the sea.

But maybe that wasn't the bottom of the barrel, after all. As a matter of fact, the next one was bound to happen. Herman Cohen, a twenty-nine-year-old producer, came out with *I Was a Teenage Werewolf* in 1957. He had studied the results of a poll that said that 70 percent of the movie-going public was within the twelve-to-twenty-five-years age range. So he decided to appeal to the young, invested one hundred fifty thousand dollars in the picture, and grossed some two million, three hundred thousand dollars in a short time.

The Curse of the Werewolf, made by Hammer in 1961, is probably the most intelligent of the wolf-man films, in spite of the fact that the fiend is perhaps too wavy-haired. It combines the horror of the werewolf story

Michael Landon, before he caught on in television's "Bonanza" series, as the hero of I Was A Teenage Werewolf *(American International, 1957).*

Oliver Reed as the monster in The Curse of the Werewolf *(Hammer, 1961).*

with an almost anthropological approach to the legends of lycanthropy. And add to that a magnificent performance by Oliver Reed as the werewolf.

These were not the only werewolf films, by any means. There were others: *The Undying Monster* (American, 1942); *Cry of the Werewolf* (American, 1944); *She-Wolf of London* (American, 1946); *The Werewolf* (American, 1956); and *Lycanthropus* (a German film of 1961, which was released in the United States as *Werewolf in a Girls' Dormitory,* and in Great Britain, for some reason or other, as *I Married a Werewolf).*

Three films were based loosely on a short story called *The Fly.* The first one, a 1958 picture entitled, naturally

David Hedison as The Fly, *in his laboratory (Twentieth Century–Fox, 1958).*

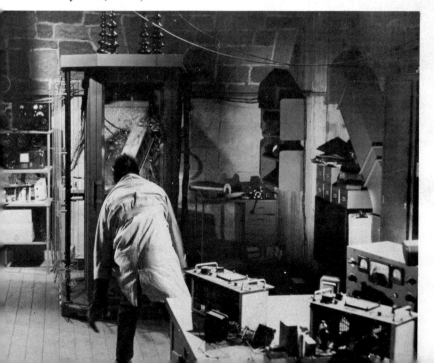

enough, *The Fly,* is the story of a scientist who develops a machine that will transport matter instantaneously from place to place. The big problem arises when he tries to transmit his own body across the width of his laboratory.

There is a fly in the ointment—a real fly in the machine, that is. At the end of the experiment, he is intact, but with the fly's head, and the fly has his. Fair enough. At the end of the film, the scientist does away with himself, with his wife's help, by squashing the ghastly head in a hydraulic press, so that no one will ever know the nature of his experimental failure. The fly with the human head ends up as a spider's dinner. By the way, nobody bothered to explain how the scientist with the fly's head was able to retain his own human brain, especially since the man's head on the fly's body was able to speak.

In the very next year came *The Return of the Fly,* in which the scientist's son tried the same experiment and became a monster, too. As we have seen with the Frankenstein family, some people never learn. Then there was *The Curse of the Fly* in 1965, and the less said about that, the better.

CHAPTER 4

THE HUMAN FIEND

*One was evidently a female. The other two were men . . .
their skins were of a dull pinkish drab colour, such as I had
seen in no savages before. They had fat heavy chinless
faces, retreating foreheads, and a scant bristly hair upon
their heads. Never before had I seen such bestial-looking
creatures. . . . Each of these creatures, despite its human
form, its rag of clothing, and the rough humanity of its
bodily form, had woven into it, into its movements, into
the expression of its countenance, into its whole presence,
some now irresistible suggestion of a hog, a swinish taint,
the unmistakable mark of the beast.*

That's a description of the work of Dr. Moreau. It comes from a story, *The Island of Dr. Moreau,* by the great science fiction writer H. G. Wells. Oh, those mad scientists! Where would horror films be without them?

The basic reason for the popularity of the movie starring a crazed doctor who runs around doing atrocious things to animals, plants, and even human beings, is a seemingly ingrained suspicion that we have toward science itself. And we come by this suspicion honestly. It's been with us for a good long time.

The early scientists were content to sit around and discuss their subject matter with each other, and so were no threat to the established beliefs of the day. But suspicion began to rear its ugly head when these learned men began to hang out in their laboratories, performing experiments that, while they were not blasphemous, at least produced results that might cause their fellow men to question long-established ideas.

The scientists were almost forced to go underground. They had to write up their experiments so that nobody but other scientists could decipher them. For example, the alchemist Zosimus, who lived about A.D. 300, set down a recipe. He told his colleagues that they must slaughter the dragon Ourobouros and thoroughly mince his blood and bones. One had to be a fellow alchemist to know that this dragon was supposed to have three ears (sulfur, arsenic, and mercury) and four legs (lead, copper, tin, and iron). And they also knew that they must smelt and burn these "ears" and "legs."

70

But what if Zosimus had not hidden his secret? There was a chance that some king or other would arrest him and try to force him to work magic—to change lead into gold, for example (remember Rumplestiltskin?). And if it were not possible to do this—"Off with his head!" The best way for a scientist to avoid this situation, therefore, was to give the king a strange formula and skip the country while the royal soothsayers were busy trying to figure out what it was that he had in mind.

Then, too, there was trouble if you went against the teachings of whatever church happened to be in power at the time. The scientists might be practicing heresy. They might be discovering things that were not a part of the ancient writings of the church, or they might be carrying on experiments in which they prayed for success. And most of the early religions insisted that all of the praying be done by the priests of the faith. So some of these early scientists were asked by their teachers to take an oath of secrecy:

> "I swear—by heaven and earth; by light and
> by darkness; by fire, water, air, and earth; by the
> height of heaven, the depth of the earth, and the
> abyss beneath the world; by Thoth and Anubis; by
> the bark of the three-headed Cerberus, the guard-
> ian of the nether-world; by Charon's ferry and by
> Charon, the ferryman; by the three goddesses of
> Necessity, by the scourge and by the sword—I
> shall reveal the secret to no one but solely to my

child and dear son, in order that he may be like you and you like he."

And then there were always the people who were just plain greedy and would want the scientists to create something that could be turned into ready cash. Usually, the devoted scientist, just as today, was not interested in that. He merely wanted to continue with his work.

Although the early alchemists made their peace with the church toward the end of the fourth century, they were still a race apart—not like other people. But for a while, even priests dabbled in science. St. Albertus Magnus and his pupil St. Thomas Aquinas are two examples. However, from time to time, some scientist or other would shoot off his mouth. And presto! He was in trouble.

Arnold of Villanova is an example. He was an alchemist of the thirteenth century who made prophesies. He predicted the death of King Peter of Aragon in 1285, and it happened that very year. He predicted the end of the world in 1335, and missed. But his prophesies began to anger the pope, who caused him to be excommunicated. His writings were banned, and he was later thrown in jail and sentenced to be burned at the stake. The only thing that saved him was the fact that the pope became ill and Arnold saved his life.

Another alchemist, Agrippa, was accused of witchcraft and thrown into prison in 1531. He was eventually released.

Gradually the scientist began to become a respected

A portrait of Albertus Magnus (left) by de Bry and one of Thomas Aquinas (right).

member of the community. There were fakes, frauds, and swindlers among the group, of course, but by the eighteenth century science was quite a common hobby even of members of the aristocracy—look at Lavoisier, Benjamin Franklin, and others. Deep down, however, the common man retains his suspicions of the man in the white laboratory jacket. Even though we applaud the results of modern science—the polio vaccine, transplant surgery, the landing on the moon—we are secretly not surprised at the failures of science: excessive chemical insecticides, radioactive pollution, the side effects of modern drugs. The scientist is still a man apart.

Other types of human fiends–mad doctors in our folk-lore were merely hypnotists. Perhaps they can trace their origins back to the eighteenth century, where their fore-runner was Dr. Franz Anton Mesmer.

An eighteenth-century caricature of Mesmer in his laboratory.

Mesmer, from whom we get our word *mesmerism,* claimed that he could cure diseases by changing the sufferer's "animal magnetism." It turned out that he was merely hypnotizing his patients.

Not that all of the human fiends were mad doctors, however. Some of them were merely insane and had no medical degree at all. In a sense, a psychotic can turn himself into a monster. But in films, these mental defectives are a comparatively recent idea. The main reason for this is that a movie study of mental illness can rarely be done without more detail and dialogue than can be got from a silent film. So the insane ones had to wait for the talking picture.

Let's turn back the clock, and turn on the projector.

Out of the popularity of mesmerism and hypnotism came the stories of the sleepwalker, or somnambulist. Here we have a monster who has been put into a deep sleep by a mad doctor and caused to do the bidding of his master. An added part of the story is that the sleepwalker has enormous strength and can feel no pain.

In 1913, Hans Janowitz, a young Czech writer, experienced something that was eventually to have a profound effect on the world of horror films. He was attending a fair in Hamburg, Germany, and noticed a strange man lurking about some bushes in a park. When he read the papers the next day he learned that there had been a brutal murder of a young girl at that same spot where he had seen the prowler. Janowitz attended the funeral of the murdered girl and again saw the mysterious man. He had no proof that the man had been the murderer, and, as far as the police were concerned, the case was never solved.

After a few years had passed, Janowitz met a young poet, a former Austrian infantry officer named Carl Mayer. He told his story to the poet, who, in turn, told Janowitz of his experiences with an army psychiatrist who had made fun of Mayer's philosophical ideas because he felt that the young officer was a mentally sick person.

So the two writers decided to collaborate on a story. They called it *The Cabinet of Dr. Caligari,* and they took it to a German film company, Delca, to show to the producer, Erich Pommer. Pommer immediately bought the script for something in the neighborhood of two hundred dollars. Before you think that Janowitz and Mayer were robbed, it should be pointed out that the story may not have been completely original. There is an old German folk tale dating from the eleventh century that told of a dishonest monk who had a sleepwalking slave committed to do his evil bidding.

At any rate, the film that emerged was one of the first pictures involving a mad scientist—Dr. Caligari. He controlled the mind of a sleepwalker and often forced him to do a bit of business that later became what seemed to be a requirement in all monster movies. The somnambulist would sneak into the heroine's bedroom and carry her off. Of course, she was always dressed in a long white robe.

The story of *The Cabinet of Dr. Caligari* starts with a traveling fair that is set up in the village of Holstenwall. Dr. Caligari, with his hypnotized somnambulist, Cesare, wants to open a fortune-telling booth. The town clerk is cruel and insulting to Dr. Caligari, and the next day the poor official is found to have been murdered. Guess who did it. Anyway, Caligari opens his booth, exhibiting Cesare, who lives in a coffinlike cabinet.

Alan and Francis, two students, attend the show in

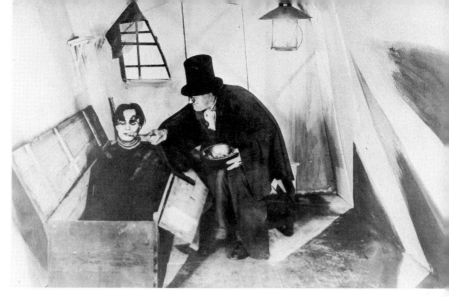

Caligari feeds the somnambulist, Cesare (above), in The Cabinet of Dr. Caligari. *Conrad Veidt is in the cabinet and Werner Krauss is the doctor (Decla-Bioscop, 1920). Courtesy* Movie Star News. *(Below) Jane appears on the scene, played by Lil Dagover, in* The Cabinet of Dr. Caligari *(Decla-Bioscop, 1920).*

Caligari's booth, and Cesare predicts that Alan will die before morning. When Alan is killed, Francis tries to convince the police that Caligari and Cesare are to blame, but they will not pay any attention to him. If they did, the story would be over before it had really begun.

Next, for some reason, Cesare is sent out to murder Francis's girlfriend, Jane. But, as you might guess, she is too beautiful to be murdered, so Cesare merely kidnaps her. Jane's vocal chords are her salvation. Attracted by her screams, a crowd starts chasing the somnambulist. He drops Jane, runs away, and dies of exhaustion and exposure in a nearby woods. Caligari then escapes, and Francis follows him.

The last part of the story reveals that Caligari is really the director of an insane asylum and is nuttier than his patients. Francis exposes him and he is put into a straitjacket.

That's the way the story went. But by the time director Robert Wiene got through with it, some changes had been made. The film opens with a scene in which Francis is sitting on a park bench, talking to an old man. Jane walks by, looking as if she were also a somnambulist. Francis explains that they have had quite an experience and begins to tell the original story.

At the end of the film, Caligari is revealed as the director of the insane asylum, all right. But Francis, Jane, and the somnambulist are patients there, and the events in the picture were merely the products of Francis's demented mind.

The film, released in 1920, was a sensation. The eerie flat black and white scenery that looked like cubist paintings and the performances of the actors (especially Werner Krauss as Caligari and Conrad Veidt as Cesare) were terrifying. The film gives to the audience a feeling of observing a horrible nightmare. This was a great picture and has been copied over and over again since it was first seen in 1920.

An example of this copycatting was a film of 1926, *The Bells.* In this one, Boris Karloff played a hypnotist who was obviously a takeoff on old *Dr. Caligari.*

Another mad doctor was played by Lon Chaney, Sr., in the 1929 film *The Monster.* The funny thing about this picture was that it was a satire about a type of movie that had not been invented yet. It was probably the first real mad scientist film. Chaney was a semicomic scientist who arranged that automobile accidents would happen near his laboratory so that he would have dead bodies to work on.

The Monster was a precursor of the film *The Raven.* In *The Raven,* released in 1935, Bela Lugosi runs a quiet little country clinic complete with an Edgar Allan Poe torture chamber in the basement. Poor Boris Karloff, an escaped criminal, hopes that Lugosi will change his face by plastic surgery. But the operation is not a complete success. One side of Karloff's face is scarred, his lips are twisted, and one eye is lower than the other. One wonders where Bela went to medical school.

H. G. Wells's great story *The Island of Dr. Moreau*

was made into a movie in 1933 and released as *The Island of Lost Souls*. Dr. Moreau was played by Charles Laughton, a talented English actor who had yet to make his big splash as Captain Bligh in the 1936 production of *Mutiny on the Bounty*.

Moreau felt called upon to change animals of all types into men and women, or reasonable facsimiles. This was done by performing horrible vivisections. The most successful of his experiments is a girl named Lola, a fine panther woman. However, she and the good doctor have disagreements because, among other things, he forgets that she has a naturally feline nature.

Now Dr. Moreau has patiently taught his animals to be gentle. Then he makes the mistake of ordering an ape man to commit murder. So the monsters discover that they are able to revolt. And revolt they do.

The leader of the beasts in *The Island of Lost Souls* is, by the way, Bela Lugosi.

Moreau is taken prisoner and hauled off into the torture chamber of a laboratory, where the animals begin to operate upon him. Turn about is fair play. But not exactly, because the whole island catches fire and the blaze destroys every living thing except the hero and heroine who, of course, are able to escape. For some reason or other, this film was banned by the censor in Great Britain. It might have been due to pressure by the Royal Society for the Prevention of Cruelty to Animals.

It is possible that a certain phrase, since become quite common, first saw the light of day in *The Island of Lost*

Souls. Laughton and his human captives are having dinner inside his fortress as the human animals are having a meeting outside. Drums are beating and low murmurs can be heard coming from the beasts. Laughton looks at his guests and utters the deathless line: "The natives are restless tonight."

The Mystery of the Wax Museum was perhaps the only important horror film ever made by Warner Brothers. It was released in 1933, and was directed by Michael Curtiz and starred another British actor, Lionel Atwill. The film tells the story of a mad artist who kills people, dips them in wax, and behold—another work of art. One of the important features of the movie was that it was shot in color. This film was remade in 1953 in 3-D. Called *House of Wax,* it starred Vincent Price.

Charles Laughton disciplining his monsters in The Island of Lost Souls *(Universal, 1933). The one with the most hair is Bela Lugosi.*

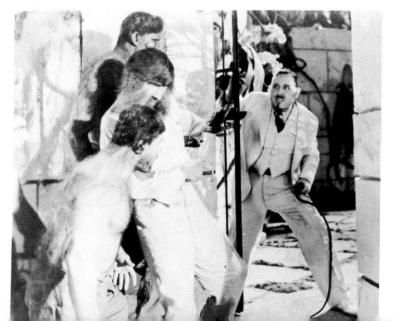

Another example of the many times that Lionel At-will played the mad scientist was the film *Man Made Monster,* released in 1941. In this picture he doses Lon Chaney, Jr. with so much electricity that he walks around in a perpetual glow and must wear a rubber suit. The monster eventually kills the scientist, carries off the girl, and dies when his suit catches on a barbed wire fence which drains him of all of his electrical energy.

Universal Studios tried to start another horror series about an ape woman named Paula Dupree. It started with *Captive Wild Woman* in 1943. Dr. Sigmund Walters (John Carradine) injects some hormones into a circus ape and then puts his lady assistant's brain into the head of the beast. The result is a beautiful girl who turns into an ape when she gets excited. But she kills Walters and eventually she herself is shot to death. Or was she? The next time around, in *Jungle Woman* (1944), Dr. Fletcher (J. Carrol Naish) brings her back to life and beauty. But the silly girl turns back into an ape again and dies.

In 1945, Dr. Stendhal (Otto Kruger) gives her corpse another transfusion in *Jungle Captive,* but she gets shot again. This time she—and the series—remained dead.

Albert Dekker, a fine stage character actor, was a moderate success in the 1940 film *Dr. Cyclops.* He played the role of Dr. Alexander Thorkel, an almost blind scientist. Thorkel fools around with radioactive material in his laboratory situated on the Amazon River. Finally, he is able to change living things in such a way that they shrink. The human dolls in his menagerie average about five or six inches in height. Naturally these little people have many death-defying encounters with cats, insects, and other perils, but they eventually kill the doctor and, wonder of wonders, end up at their normal height again.

Now, on with the psychotic monsters. Few of these people actually turn themselves into monsters. A couple of exceptions are *The Invisible Man* and the hero of *Psycho.*

Boris Karloff pulled essentially the same kind of stunt that Bela Lugosi had previously pulled when the time came for James Whale to film H. G. Wells's ghoulish novelette *The Invisible Man.* Karloff didn't want to be invisible until the end of the picture, and so the part was given to Claude Rains. This launched Rains's movie career in much the same way as Lugosi's turning down the Frankenstein monster role was so helpful to Karloff.

The 1933 film, *The Invisible Man,* is the story of a mysterious stranger who turns up in a small English village. His hands are encased in gloves and his head is completely covered with bandages. He wears a pair of dark glasses. The man seems to be a chemist who is diligently looking for an unknown formula.

It turns out that the man is a Dr. Griffen, who has discovered a batch of chemicals that will turn flesh and bone and blood to a state of invisibility. Unfortunately, it also makes the subject insane. Griffen is full of plans to dominate the world. He derails trains, robs banks, and murders people—all in his invisible state. When he is finally caught and shot, he returns to visibility.

Claude Rains as The Invisible Man, *with Gloria Stuart (Universal, 1933).*

The trick photography in this film was fantastic. Imagine watching a man unwind the bandages around his head and finding that there is nothing underneath to be seen. The transformation in *The Invisible Man* was probably done with a combination of double exposure (exposing the film twice) and masked negative (blotting out the exposure of the man's head on the film and letting the second half of the double exposure shine through). This trick was picked up again in *The Invisible Man Returns,* starring Vincent Price (1940).

One of the best films about an out-and-out nut case was Alfred Hitchcock's *Psycho,* made in 1960. A young girl steals some money from her employer, drives away in her car, and ends up in a small motel located next door to a creepy old house. The motel is run by a charming young man named Norman (Tony Perkins) who lives in the nearby house where he looks after his invalid mother.

Then it would seem that Norman's mother is not as sick as we thought. She kills the young girl by stabbing her to death. Norman comes back to clean up the mess and deposits everything—body, luggage, and automobile—in a convenient bed of quicksand. When a detective noses around, he, too, is stabbed to death by the mother.

But it turns out that the mother is long dead, and that Norman is keeping her mummified body in the cellar of the house. You see, Norman has been, from time to time, putting on his mother's dresses and imitating her voice, manners, and personality whenever he is out on a rampage. When he commits the murders in this movie, no wonder that the local police are baffled.

Psycho was successful because it was beautifully edited, giving the audience surprise after surprise. The exotic heroine is killed off in the first half hour of the film, Anthony Perkins looks too nice to be a murderer, and the detective is much too efficient to be ambushed. This was Hitchcock's finest horror picture.

CHAPTER 5

BACK FROM THE DEAD

His face was a strong—a very strong—aquiline, with high bridge of the thin nose and peculiarly arched nostrils; with lofty domed forehead, and hair growing scantily around the temples but profusely elsewhere. His eyebrows were very massive, almost meeting over the nose, and with bushy hair that seemed to curl in its own profusion. The mouth, so far as I could see it under the heavy moustache, was fixed and rather cruel-looking, with peculiarly sharp white teeth; these protruded over the lips, whose remarkable ruddiness showed astonishing vitality in a man of his years. For the rest, his ears were pale, and at tops extremely pointed; the chin was broad and strong, and the cheeks firm though thin. The general effect was

*one of extraordinary pallor. . . . Hitherto I had noticed the
backs of his hands . . . and they had seemed rather white
and fine; but seeing them now close to me, I could not but
notice that they were rather coarse—broad, with squat
fingers. . . . There were hairs in the center of the palm.
The nails were long and fine, and cut to a sharp point.*

That's what a vampire is supposed to look like, according to Bram Stoker, the author of the novel *Dracula.*
And these horrible ghosts are said to rise from the grave
during the night and wander around looking for victims
to bite. They always seem to be hungry and they drink
people's blood.

The legend of the vampire dates back at least to ancient Greece. At that time, there were supposed to be
female creatures called Empusas who were always looking for husbands. They must have been the praying man-
tids of their day, since as soon as they married some poor
man, they would suck out all of his blood.

At the same time, the Greeks had the Lamia. This was
also a type of beautiful woman. She would drink blood
when she wasn't busy removing her eyes in order to
frighten people.

Those Greeks had some imagination. Add to the Em-
pusa and the Lamia the ghosts known as Striges. They
were the ones who picked on children. Not by marrying
them, of course. The Strige would turn into a bird, fly into
a nursery, and feed off a little tot's blood.

In France, during the fifth and sixth centuries, some laws were passed against vampirism, and the French church recommended excommunication. But our typical vampire is pretty much a Balkan invention. The belief was developed there during the sixteenth century. By the beginning of the seventeenth century, the vampire legend had begun to spread throughout most of Europe.

Gustave Doré used frightening bat people to populate hell in this illustration from Dante's Inferno.

No. 1.] Nos. 2, 3 and 4 are Presented, Gratis, with this No. [Price 1d.
VARNEY
THE
VAMPIRE.
OR THE
FEAST OF BLOOD
A ROMANCE OF EXCITING INTEREST.
BY THE AUTHOR OF
"GRACE RIVERS; OR, THE MERCHANT'S DAUGHTER."
LONDON: E. LLOYD, SALISBURY-SQUARE, AND ALL BOOKSELLERS.

The frontispiece from an 1847 vampire novel.

The poets and novelists, however, have kept the stories coming. Goethe, Lord Byron, and Southey all wrote poems about the blood drinkers. Alexandre Dumas wrote a vampire play in the 1850s. In 1853, a pulp magazine type of book appeared called *Varney the Vampire,* which was enormously successful. And then, in 1897, along came the novel *Dracula* by Bram Stoker, which has since been the basis for so many movies.

The vampire is usually thin and corpselike. He can be seen wearing the clothing in which he was buried, normal street clothes, or a well-tailored suit of evening clothes. If you ever should run into a fat vampire, you may be sure that he has just had his midnight snack.

He is said to have thick, red lips, and his teeth are long and sharp. You may not notice the latter, since it's a long time between smiles for a vampire. Some Russians used to believe that the vampire's teeth are made of steel and can also be used to chomp his way out of his coffin.

Naturally, his skin is white and cold. He's dead, you know. His eyes may gleam red, his hands are hairy, his eyebrows are bushy, and his fingernails need clipping. Add to all of this his immense strength, pointed ears, and bad breath.

This is not a completely standard description, however. Some Bulgarians used to say that the vampire has but a single nostril. And there were Polish people a few years back who said that his tongue was pointed, and others who said that it had a barb on the end.

The vampire can live forever, unless he is killed in the ritual way. He does not throw a shadow and he casts no reflection in a mirror. He can change into an animal or even into a bit of fog. And he can't stand running water.

As everyone knows, the vampire must remain in his coffin from dawn to nightfall, although there are some

An old painting, The Resuscitated Corpse, *from the Wiertz Museum .*

Greeks who believe that he can't come out to play on Friday. That day is the day when it is best to dig up graves in the hope of finding a fiend. When you find one, he will be helpless.

Suppose that you want to become a vampire. The easiest way is to find a vampire and let him bite you. No one knows just how many times this must happen—some say once, some say several times. A few people believe that if one dies in a state of sin, he will become a vampire,

91

but if that were true, there would be a lot more vampires around.

In some countries, it is believed that if a vampire looks at a pregnant woman, her child will become a vampire, too. Or, if a child dies without being baptized—zap! And lying to one's parents is thought to be another way.

But the problem is not how to become a vampire, rather how to get rid of one that is not welcome in the house. Garlic and hawthorn branches are said to be good for this. Religious articles, such as a crucifix or a consecrated host from the church, should also work, although it is hard to believe that all vampires are Christian. Marking a cross in tar on your front door should help, too.

If you happen to find the grave of a vampire, you can run iron stakes through the coffin straight into the ground. Or you can bury the body under running water.

So you tried to keep him away, but he won't play fair. The only thing left to do is to kill him. A silver bullet may do the job, but you had better have it blessed by a priest first. The most common way is to drive a stake through the vampire's heart. To be on the safe side, use an aspen or white thorn stake and drive it in with a single blow. Other recommendations to supplement the stake are to break the neck of the vampire, to cut off his head, to cut his leg muscles and stick pins into his calves and thighs. It is said that in certain parts of old Russia and Poland, the villagers made a paste of the vampire's body and then sat down and ate the paste.

Another popular movie character who comes back from the dead is the mummy. The ancient Egyptians believed that the physical body was essential to the human personality, and a dead person could not go on to an afterlife without it. So they had to preserve the corpse as best they could.

When the Egyptians began to experiment with mummification, the body was merely wrapped with linen bandages so that it would not fall apart. Then they began to treat the body with salt or a type of soda, and wrap it in bandages treated with resin. Even the fingers were bandaged separately.

Along about the third century B.C., the embalmers were able to remove or shrink much of the flesh from the bodies before mummification. Mummies from this period are dark-colored and have brittle skin. In the second century B.C., the Egyptians had opened new trade routes and the embalmers were able to use new spices and medicines from Africa and the Middle East. The results were beautifully preserved bodies, some of them with artificial eyes, and most of them with packing inside that filled out the features and the body itself in order that it might look more lifelike.

Then there is the zombie. According to an American writer, W. B. Seabrook, a zombie is "a soulless human corpse, still dead, but taken from the grave and endowed by sorcery with a mechanical semblance of life."

Seabrook actually claimed to have seen these poor creatures working in the fields of Haiti and described them as dull and plodding, "with the eyes of a dead man, not blind, but staring, unfocused, unseeing."

It is said that people who believe in zombies will guard the grave of a dead relative for quite a while—until they are sure that the body has begun to rot away. The explanation is that a magician cannot turn a decayed corpse into a zombie. And he wants to own a zombie so that this ghost will work for him and obey his bidding without resistance.

The creation of a zombie supposedly begins when the sorcerer gets on a horse and then rides backwards to the house of the victim. What if the poor unfortunate is still alive? No problem. The magician can get him by sucking out his soul through a crack in the door. Just blow the soul into a container, and he's got him trapped.

Then the victim dies and is buried. When the sorcerer digs up the body, he holds the open bottle under the nose of the corpse and has his zombie. Some say that all that is necessary is for the magician to get hold of a fresh corpse—soul or no soul.

To protect the body from this magic, in addition to guarding the grave, you can plant the corpse under cement, or bury it in a busy place where any sorcerer will be caught doing his dirty work. There are people who swear by the method of burial in which a dagger is put into the hand of the dead one so that he will be able to protect himself from the magician.

And if you run across a zombie and want it to return to its grave, all you have to do is feed him a little meat or

94

salt. He then remembers that he is supposed to be dead and buried and goes back to the cemetery.

Vampires, walking mummies, zombies—all of them have become popular with the makers of monster movies, and the viewers of monster movies, too. But the funny thing about these three types of creatures from the dead is that very few people really believe in them any more. Actually, there is a great deal of doubt that very many people ever believed in them. Ignorant peasants believed in witches and werewolves, but our three types of walking dead were never that much of a threat.

It was the fiction writers who did the dirty work. Only when a new novel was published about vampires and zombies would stories of their existence pop up in the papers. And the Egyptians never did believe that their carefully preserved mummies could get up and walk through the land of the living.

Let's roll the projector.

The first of all of the screen vampires appeared in *The Devil's Castle,* made by Georges Méliès in France. This beauty of 1896 ends as a gentleman holds up a crucifix and the fiend gives up and disappears.

The film didn't seem to have much impact, since the next vampire movie, a German production, wasn't released until 1922 in Europe and 1929 in the United States. It was called *Nosferatu,* and was directed by Friedrich Wilhelm Murnau.

The Bram Stoker novel *Dracula* had been published only twenty-five years before *Nosferatu* was made, and the copyright was still in effect. So, in order not to have to pay money to the Stoker estate, some changes were made. The main action of the story occurs in Bremen, Germany—not in London. The time of the story was switched from the 1890s back to the 1830s. The vampire's name was changed from Count Dracula to Count Orlock. Also the film was renamed *Nosferatu,* which means "The Undead."

But essentially the story was the same. A young clerk is sent to Transylvania in order to settle some business with a nobleman. He arrives at a spooky old castle and is greeted by the count, who turns out to be a vampire. The clerk spends the night and the next day finds his host laid out in a coffin in a secret room of the castle. But he also finds out that he is the count's prisoner.

Presumably the count has drained the Transylvanian peasants of most of their blood, so he leaves for Bremen. Count Orlock also takes the black plague with him to Bremen, as if vampirism weren't enough.

Then the clerk escapes. He races back to Bremen and notifies the people of the vampire's imminent arrival by sea.

In the book, as Dracula is committing his crimes in London, a great many people are involved in tracking him down. Among them is a wise Dutch scientist, Professor Van Helsing, who eventually is able to trace the vampire to his coffin and kill him with a stake through his heart. But in *Nosferatu,* the wife of the clerk handles the whole thing by herself in Bremen.

Her shortcut is to entice Orlock to her room and let him feast off her blood. Then she holds him there until the cock crows in the morning. Alas, she dies with Orlock. All in all, *Nosferatu* turned out to be a real thriller.

The star of the film was a German actor billed as Max Schreck, but who could believe that? *Schreck* means "terror" in German, and there are those who think that the actor was really another performer by the name of Alfred Abel. At any rate, Orlock was a terrifying figure—tall, thin, with incredibly long fingernails, sharp teeth, and a bald head like a rat's.

In *London after Midnight,* a 1927 film, Lon Chaney, Sr. did not play the vampire as a sophisticated nobleman. He had a sort of insane look about him—wide, staring eyes with circles all around them, teeth filed to fine points, white, unkempt hair. He wandered around in a black cloak, white tie, and top hat.

Chaney suffered in his makeup for this movie. He used thin wires to make his eyes bulge and wore a set of false animal teeth that he could put up with for only a very short time before the pain would get the better of him.

The first vampire that talked was played by Bela Lugosi in the 1931 Universal picture, *Dracula.* Although it was an American picture, about the only prominent American involved was the great director, Tod Browning, who had made many films starring the old master, Lon Chaney, Sr. The selection of the story was made by a German story editor, the movie was photographed by a German cameraman, and it starred the Hungarian

Max Schreck as the terrifying Orlock
(Prana, 1922).

A poster announcing the first talking Dracula, from a novel by
Abraham [sic] Stoker (Universal, 1931).

99

Lugosi, who was forever after to be identified with the role of Count Dracula.

Universal had decided to make a film based on Stoker's novel, and had intended to have Browning and Chaney team up again. But Chaney, the master of horror, died of cancer before shooting could begin. He was therefore replaced by Arisztid Olt, the actor who had changed his name to the less tongue-twisting Bela Lugosi. Lugosi had played the count before, on the Broadway stage, in a production of a play called, oddly enough, *Dracula.*

Lugosi was great. He seemed to believe that he was a vampire from the first moment when he announced to the horrified hero of the film, "I am—Dracula!" Not that the script writer didn't give Dracula a sense of humor. At dinner he announces to the other guests, "I never drink —wine."

In the film we see a young man named Renfield riding in a carriage on his way to Castle Dracula. It is an eerie place, a ruin filled with cobwebs. It has huge staircases and cold fireplaces. Renfield meets Dracula and soon discovers that he is a vampire. Of course Dracula soon turns the young man into a vampire. Renfield ends up eating flies and cackling to himself.

The evil count has trouble getting a meal, since he has run out of people in the neighborhood to bite. So he packs up and takes a ship to England. He terrorizes a few people, turning a young girl named Lucy into a vampire, for example, but is finally killed by Dr. Van Helsing, the vampire expert.

Lugosi walks out of the cobwebs of Castle Dracula in Dracula *(Universal, 1931).*

There were a few good touches in the second part of the movie. One of them was a scene in which the normal people realize that Dracula does not cast a reflection in a silver box. But most of the horrible things that happen— Dracula's arrival in the form of a mist, his death by a stake in the heart—happen offscreen. After the excellent first section of the film with all of its mysterious scenery and its creepy characters such as the weird coachman and the pasty-faced vampire girls living in the castle, the second part seems drab.

Would you believe that *Dracula* had its premiere on St. Valentine's Day?

The next year, 1932, another Dracula film was released. This was *Vampyr*, made in France by the Danish director Carl Dreyer. Although the script by Sheridan Le Fanu was more poetic than the Browning version, it was more slow moving.

But Dreyer wanted atmosphere and he got it. He is quoted as saying to his cameraman:

> "Imagine we are sitting in an ordinary room. Suddenly we are told that there is a corpse behind the door. In an instant the room we are sitting in is completely altered: everything in it has taken on another level: the light, the atmosphere have changed, though they are physically the same. This is because *we* have changed, and the objects *are* as we conceive them. This is the effect I want to get."

Whenever the action in this movie was involved with supernatural happenings, a fine gauze filter was placed several feet in front of the lens. This gave a weird glow to objects and made the actors appear indistinct, as though they were moving about in a constant twilight.

Lugosi and Browning came back in 1935 with *The Mark of the Vampire,* in which there was also a female vampire. Dracula was never known to have married, and even when he seemed attracted to a girl, it was purely for biting purposes. So it probably would have been a surprise to him, had he lived, to hear about the next two films.

Dracula's Daughter, billed as "more sensational than her unforgettable father," came along in 1936. Countess Marya Zaleska invites a scientist to her Transylvanian castle, and strange things happen. In the end, when her slave tries to kill the scientist with an arrow, Marya steps in front of him and gets the wooden shaft through the heart. That's all she needed to be killed.

Lon Chaney, Jr. turned up as the *Son of Dracula* in 1943. There is not much to say about the artistic merits of this film. Chaney was not the suave gentleman that his father was, in spite of cleverly operating under the alias of Anthony Alucard (spell that one backwards). But Chaney had had so much practice in changing into a wolf that this time the producers let him change into a bat. The coffin is found and burned and Alucard cannot find a place to lay his weary head. So he is killed by the sunrise.

We have already mentioned John Carradine's two go-rounds with the role of Dracula. In *The House of Fran-*

103

kenstein (1944) he seemed to be finished off. But he looked healthy again in *The House of Dracula* (1945), although a cure for his vampirism was never found. Then Bela Lugosi came back for a curtain call in *Abbott and Costello Meet Frankenstein* where, as Dracula, he is caught, in bat form, by the Wolf Man.

As was the case with *Frankenstein,* Hammer Studios in England then took over. In 1958, Terence Fisher directed *Dracula,* released in the United States as *The Horror of Dracula,* starring Christopher Lee as the everlasting count. In this one, Peter Cushing, as Van Helsing, got him with a crucifix and Dracula turned into dust.

Vampires can be found in Mexico, too. A hungry Count Duval, played by Germán Robles, eyes Adriana Welter in El Vampiro *(Abel Salazar/Cinematográfica A.B.S.A., 1959).*

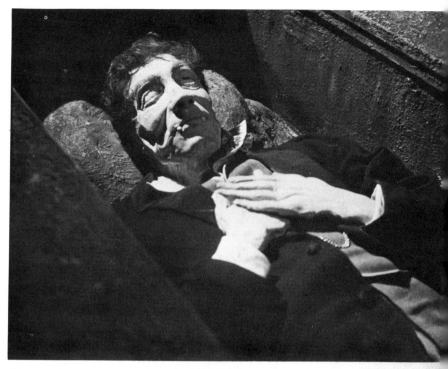

Christopher Lee got his just deserts in The Horror of Dracula *(Hammer, 1958).*

But you can't keep a good vampire down. In 1965 Lee played *Dracula, Prince of Darkness*. Someone had bled on his ashes and revived the count. This time he was killed by running water—a nice switch. In *Dracula Has Risen From the Grave* in 1968, he defied death again.

But in case you think that that takes care of the Dracula films, you're wrong. Many other vampire movies have been made over the years. Here are some of them:

- *The Devil Bat* (with Lugosi, American, 1940); *The Return of the Vampire* (with Lugosi, American, 1943); *Dead Men Walk* (American, 1943); *The Vampire's Ghost* (American, 1945); *Devil Bat's Daughter* (American, 1946); *My Son the Vampire* (with Lugosi, British, original title: *Mother Riley Meets the Vampire,* 1952); *The Vampire* (American, 1957); *I Vampiri* (Italian, English title: *Lust of the Vampires,* 1957); *Blood of Dracula* (American, 1957); *The Return of Dracula* (American, 1958); *Blood of the Vampire* (British, 1958); *Brides of Dracula* (British, 1960); *Kiss of the Vampire* (British, 1962); *Black Sabbath* (with Karloff, Italian, 1963); *Planet of the Vampires* (Italian, 1965); *Billy the Kid Versus Dracula* (American, 1965); *The Fearless Vampire Killers* (British, 1967); *Vampire Lovers* (British, 1970), as well as several Mexican, Italian, and French entries.

In 1932 the cameraman Karl Freund turned his hand to directing movies. He teamed with Boris Karloff to do *The Mummy.* This human form, though dead for centuries, made one of the most eerie movie monsters when it rose from its sarcophagus. Freund had been the photographer of *Dracula,* and previously, in Germany, of *The Golem.* Karloff got another splendid makeup job from Jack Pierce in this production.

The basic story of *The Mummy* involves an ancient Egyptian of the lower class of priests, Im-ho-tep, who falls in love with the Princess Anck-es-en-Amon. The princess dies, and Im-ho-tep tries to get the Scroll of Thoth from the temple in order to bring her back to life. But the

106

priests and the pharaoh are put out by this and sentence the poor man to be buried alive—denying him his funeral service. So he spends the next few centuries guarding his sweetheart's mummy.

Little does Bramwell Fletcher (left) suspect that Boris Karloff will soon come out of the coffin to pay him a visit as The Mummy *(Universal, 1932).*

The rest of the film takes place in modern times. We see the still-living Im-ho-tep in the disguise of a terribly wrinkled Egyptian scholar, Ardath Bey. The body of the princess is taken to a museum in Cairo, and Ardath Bey tries to bring her back to life with the Scroll of Thoth. But he is discovered before he can bring this off.

Bey then finds a beautiful young girl named Helen, and for some reason he believes her to be the reincarnation of his lost love. When he approaches her to explain this idea, she calls upon the goddess Isis for help. The goddess conveniently hears the prayer, and turns the old man to dust.

Karloff played a dual role in the film—the mummy of Im-ho-tep and Ardath Bey.

Then, in 1940, Universal Studios decided to bring the mummy back. They again selected a minor cowboy actor (remember Glen Strange in the Frankenstein remake?), Tom Tyler, to be the monster. Tyler did not play a dual role in this film, *The Mummy's Hand,* he was just the mummy.

A few other changes were made. Im-ho-tep has been promoted to prince, and his name has been changed to Kharis. The princess is no longer called Anck-es-en-Amon, but Ananka. Then, too, Kharis had not stolen the Scroll of Thoth, but rather some precious tana leaves. The leaves would supposedly bring the dead back to life. He was not only buried alive, but also had had his tongue cut off.

Two scientists arrive and find the tomb of the princess and the mummy of Kharis. They decide to take

108

Ananka back to America, but before they can get away, Kharis kills one of them. The other scientist succeeds in taking the princess to a museum in a small New England town.

Meanwhile, back in Egypt, the High Priest of the Temple of Amon-Ra prepares to take Kharis to America so that the body of Ananka can be returned to her tomb. The High Priest (George Zucco) is careful to take a supply of tana leaves with him to feed to the mummy. The fluid from three leaves will keep Kharis alive, while the fluid from nine will permit him to move and give him tremendous strength. The two of them arrive in New England and, although Kharis is able to kill a few people, he is eventually destroyed by fire.

As you might expect, Lon Chaney, Jr. got his chance at the mummy, too. In 1942 he appeared in *The Mummy's Tomb*. The High Priest (George Zucco again) is now an ancient man, so he must appoint a new leader. Turhan Bey is the man. Kharis, of course, is badly maimed from his experience with the fire, but by the time Bey arrives in New England, the mummy is up to trying to get Ananka back to Egypt again.

In the meantime, the new High Priest has fallen in love with a local girl and sends Kharis, the mummy, after her. The usual thing happens. The villagers come after them with torches, and the building goes up in flames, as does the mummy.

Zucco never gave up. In 1944, in *The Mummy's Ghost,* he made John Carradine the High Priest. Anaka's mummy is on display in the museum, and the High Priest takes Kharis (Lon Chaney, Jr.) there. Kharis touches Ananka, who crumbles to dust.

The High Priest and the mummy find a young college girl—an exchange student from Egypt—whom they think is the reincarnation of Ananka. Add to that the fact that the High Priest has fallen in love with her, and it is obviously the time to send Kharis after her. He plans to feed the girl (and himself) on tana leaves and make them both immortal.

Kharis doesn't think much of this plan, but he does kidnap the girl. Then he turns on the priest, kills him, grabs the girl again, and heads for the swamp. As he stumbles along, the girl in his arms changes into an ancient old hag, and they both disappear in quicksand.

Lon Chaney, Jr. also starred in *The Mummy's Curse,* made in 1944. The scene is the same swamp, now drained, twenty-five years later. Peter Coe has been named as the new High Priest and gives Kharis some tana leaves. Ananka returns from the swamp in the form of a young girl. Kharis carries her to an abandoned monastery, where the caretaker tries to make love to her. Kharis can't stand this and pulls the building down on them as Ananka turns into a mummy again.

Abbott and Costello Meet the Mummy was released in 1954.

Then came that beautiful double-play combination from Hammer Studios—*The Mummy* (1959) and *The Curse of the Mummy's Tomb* (1964). Christopher Lee is

Kharis. A scientist has shipped the mummy of Ananka to London in 1895. Kharis is revived by the Scroll of Thoth and goes after Ananka.

Lee, as The Mummy, *attacking Peter Cushing, who plays the scientist (Hammer, 1959).*

111

Bela Lugosi as the evil White Zombie *(Amusement Securities, 1932).*

But the scientist's wife turns out to be Ananka's reincarnation, so Kharis picks her up and carries her to a swamp. The mummy is shot dead and all is well.

There have been other mummy pictures, of course. Here are some of them: *The Mummy* (American, 1911); *The Dust of Egypt* (American, 1915); *The Mummy's Shroud* (British, 1967), as well as German and French films and a whole series of "Aztec Mummy" flicks from Mexico.

Zombies have not done well in the movies. Probably

the first film about them was *White Zombie,* made in 1932, starring Bela Lugosi. But he wasn't a zombie, he was Legendre, the master of the living dead. The heroine, Madge Bellamy, watches some Haitians bury a body at a crossroads so that it cannot be possessed by a sorcerer. A bunch of zombies appear on their way to the sugarcane fields.

Madge then gets married, but on her wedding night Lugosi drugs her so that even her husband thinks that she is dead. Lugosi revives her and takes her to his castle, telling his bodyguard, who is a zombie, to kill her husband. This film has a great ending. The husband escapes

Frances Dee leads the planter's wife through the forest in I Walked with a Zombie *(RKO, 1943).*

and throws Lugosi over a cliff, and all of the faithful zombies jump over the cliff after him.

I Walked with a Zombie (1943) took place in the Haitian cane fields. Frances Dee is a young nurse hired to look after a planter's wife, who is ill. The people on the island think that she is a zombie. The high point of the film is when the nurse takes the wife through the dark forests to ask the aid of the local voodoo priest.

There was a platoon of Cambodian zombies in *Revolt of the Zombies* in 1936, and a bunch of Roman zombies in *War of the Zombies* in 1963. The latter was an Italian production that starred John Drew Barrymore, the son of John Barrymore of Jekyll and Hyde fame.

Zombies were transplanted to Cornwall, in England, by Hammer Studios. This was in *Plague of the Zombies* in 1966. But these were working a tin mine instead of a sugarcane field. The tin mine exploded and all were lost.

And here are some other zombie films: *The Ghost Breakers* (American, 1940); *King of the Zombies* (American, 1941); *Bowery at Midnight* (American, 1942, with Lugosi); *The Voodoo Man* (American, 1944, with Lugosi); *Zombies on Broadway* (American, 1945, with Lugosi); *Valley of the Zombies* (American, 1946); *Voodoo Island* (American, 1957, with Karloff); *Zombies of Mora-Tau* (American, 1957); *Plan 9 from Outer Space* (American, 1958, with Lugosi); *Dr. Blood's Coffin* (British, 1960); *The Incredibly Strange Creatures Who Stopped Living and Became Mixed-up Zombies* (American, 1965); *Terror Creatures from the Grave* (Italian, 1965).

114

CHAPTER 6

THINGS FROM ANOTHER WORLD

I presently saw something stirring within the shadow: greyish billowy movements, one above another, and then two luminous disks—like eyes. Then something resembling a little grey snake, about the thickness of a walking-stick, coiled up out of the writhing middle, and wriggled in the air toward me—and then another. . . . A big greyish rounded bulk, the size, perhaps, of a bear, was rising slowly and painfully out of the cylinder. As it bulged up and caught the light, it glistened like wet leather. . . . Two large dark-coloured eyes were regarding me steadfastly. The mass that framed them, the head of the thing, it was rounded, and had, one might say, a face. There was a mouth under the eyes, the lipless brim of which quivered and panted, and dropped saliva. The whole creature heaved and pulsated convulsively. A lank tentacular appendage gripped the edge of the cylinder, another swayed in the air.

And that was the way the Martians looked as they climbed out of their invading rocket ship in H. G. Wells's *The War of the Worlds.*

It seems as though there has always been some sort of huge prehistoric monster hanging around, throwing fear into the hearts and minds of unsophisticated peasants. Over four thousand years ago, there was Ea, the fish god, who was worshipped by the ancient Babylonians. He was a good guy, however, half man and half fish, who had come up out of the sea to teach the alphabet to the people.

Ea may have been the first example of the mermaid, the merman, or the triton. These creatures were part of the ancient Hindu, Greek, and Roman tradition.

Western Europe got into the act in the sixteenth century. A monkfish monster was reported to be swimming off the coast of Norway. Later there were reports of a bishopfish in the same vicinity. Supposedly these two things had the appearance of certain members of the clergy.

Also in the sixteenth century, a French explorer sent a sea serpent to his king. It was described as having "seven heades . . . [with faces] which both in view and judgement seem more human than brutal."

The capturing of these pleasant little creatures went on. Mermen were found by a Dutch sea captain in 1663. One was found near Italy in 1684, and Queen Anne of England was said to have had one at court.

A French one was found in 1820, and a Japanese one was on view in Capetown, South Africa, in 1882. However, most of these reports can be written off by saying that these were really deformed human children or adults.

But there are stories of giant prehistoric monsters— usually sea serpents. Aristotle, in ancient Greece, wrote of one that capsized ships off the coast of Libya.

Norwegians sighted a seventy-five-foot-long creature in 1522. And the Swedes, not to be outdone by their neighbors, reported a sea monster two hundred feet long in 1555. It was described as having a lion's mane and fiery eyes, and was completely covered with scales. When this one got tired of sinking ships it would merely stand on its tail and grab sailors off the decks.

A Norwegian missionary sighted one creature off the coast of Greenland in 1734, taller than the mast of a ship, and in 1746 a Norwegian captain saw something that had the head of a horse.

It is possible that the English, the Scottish, and the Americans became tired of this Scandinavian supremacy. At any rate, they began finding monsters of their own. The lion-headed serpent was sighted again in 1848 off

Gloucester, Massachusetts, by the captain and the crew of H.M.S. *Daedalus,* and they followed it for about twenty minutes. This same beast was then seen in the South Atlantic by the men of the American brig *Daphne.*

Other sightings occurred off Scotland in 1872, off Sicily in 1877, in a Scottish lake in 1893, off Brazil in 1905, off Iceland in 1917, and off North Carolina in 1947.

But the champion of all may well be the Loch Ness Monster. The story of the creature from the depths of this large Scottish lake goes back about four hundred years to, when a missionary, St. Columba, first saw it. It has been seen, off and on, by many people over the years, and, while there are scoffers, scientists are still trying to figure out just what it was that these people have seen.

It may be that these monsters are just large eel larvae. They may be optical illusions caused by a long line of turtles swimming through the ocean. Or there may be other explanations. But the main thing is that human beings seem to want to believe in fantastic types of creatures. Even the Russians have found one of their own. It was seen by geologists in 1965, swimming in Lake Haiyr, in Siberia.

At any rate, legendary monsters were about all that

Two sketches of a sea serpent sighted off Galveston, Texas, in 1872.

A sixteenth-century woodcut showing a monster with a human head and a dragon's body.

we had to be afraid of in our films and folklore until 1945, when the atom bomb shoved us into the atomic age. Beginning with the late 1940s, the United States began its space program, and people began to be interested in life on other worlds.

These other worlds, of course, just might be populated with strange beings. These strange beings might come to visit us, or we might go to visit them. And what could be more frightening? Suppose that these other worlds did not content themselves with our natural laws? For example, suppose that there was no death there, or suppose that living things on other planets did not have the same appearance or chemical makeup that we do?

Then, too, we began to worry about the effects of radiation after the bombings of Hiroshima and Nagasaki. We learned about mutants and dehumanized creatures,

119

and these monsters began to take the place of zombies and the other forms of the living dead in our folklore.

Just as we have always been prone to believe in the strange fantastic monster, now we learn to fear the monster from another world and the monster created by radioactive mistake. Lower the house lights. Here come the films.

One of the first films that gave audiences a look-see at prehistoric monsters was the 1925 movie *The Lost World.* This had been adapted from a story by Sir Arthur Conan Doyle, the creator of Sherlock Holmes. It was the tale of a scientific expedition to the jungles of the Amazon River.

The party discovers a long-forgotten plateau. After the members of the group climb to the top of the table-land, they discover ancient giant lizards. There is also an ape man living there who they think might be the missing link that will explain the evolution of man.

The real stars of the film were the dinosaurs. These beasts had been created by a man who was to make his mark in horror films and become the dean of special effects men for many years—Willis H. O'Brien. He had made a picture in 1917, called *The Dinosaur and The Missing Link,* which the Edison Company bought for five thousand dollars and released. It lasted for only five minutes on the screen, but it had taken two months to make. O'Brien had created the animals out of modeling clay and had used stop-motion photography to give them animation.

120

O'Brien made ten films for Edison over the next few years. But for *The Lost World,* produced by First National–Watterson R. Rothacker, he gave up the clay technique and shifted to rubber models that could be made to move. Then the human characters were photographed against a backdrop of the dinosaur antics. *The Lost World* may have been the first film to tell the story of a strange beast who goes to the city. In the movie, a brontosaurus runs through the streets of London.

In 1960, when O'Brien was seventy years old, his work was still on display in the remake of *The Lost World,* which substituted real lizards for puppets. Strangely enough, the living animals did not have the personality of the rubber mannikins. But the cost of photographing the models, one frame at a time, would have been exorbitant. Salaries had gone up in the meantime, and this type of movie making can take months. The producers just did not have enough money to spend on such an activity.

The result is that the animation done in the Japanese films of today is often better than that of the monster movies in other countries. In Japan the cost of labor is much lower than in most other countries, and film makers can still use the old stop-motion techniques.

Perhaps the greatest monster movie of all time opened at Radio City Music Hall in New York City in 1933. It was *King Kong,* the brainchild of several fine film minds. Merian C. Cooper had been in Africa shooting a documentary and became interested in gorillas. He was the one who thought up the idea of a huge gorilla—a pretty intelligent one—who escapes into the streets of New York City.

He also dreamed up a setting in which the gorilla would be surrounded by prehistoric monsters and have fights with them. Cooper thought that he could film live gorillas and lizards, using trick photography.

In 1931 David O. Selznick (who was later to be responsible for *Gone with the Wind)* was a vice-president in charge of production at RKO. He brought Cooper in to do *King Kong.* In the meantime, Cooper had become familiar with the work of Willis O'Brien and changed his mind. He decided to film *King Kong* in the studio, using models.

Cooper, with his co-director, Ernest B. Schoedsack, and with O'Brien as the special effects man, started the movie in 1932. The filming took one year and cost six hundred fifty thousand dollars. But it was worth it.

The models used in the film averaged sixteen inches in height and they were truly lifelike. First the model was set up and one frame of the film was exposed. Then the model's position was slightly changed, and another frame was exposed. This was so complicated that each step that Kong takes required twelve exposures and it took one whole day to photograph a half minute of film.

When the animal shots were finished, the human actors took their places in front of a screen on which the animal action was projected from the rear. The humans then were photographed combined with the whole action of the monsters. A full-sized torso and hand of King Kong,

122

were created to be used in close-ups where he grabs the beautiful heroine, for example.

Kong was, oddly enough, both human and sympathetic. He met a horrible death while protecting Fay Wray. Yet he was probably the most terrifying of all the giant monsters.

The story is a simple one. A producer of movies, Carl Denham (Robert Armstrong), hears of a far-off island where prehistoric animals live. He discovers a beautiful, down-and-out girl (Fay Wray), who is so hungry that she consents to star in a film whose supporting characters are huge monsters. Every other actress in town has turned Denham down, and who can blame them?

The movie crew sails to Skull Island only to find that it is inhabited by a tribe of natives who are restricted to a small peninsula on the end of the island because they have built an enormous wall across the neck of the peninsula in order to keep out the monsters. One of the monsters is the tremendous gorilla, Kong. Now the natives have never seen a blond girl before, and think that poor Fay is quite unusual. So they immediately seize her, tie her up outside the wall, and declare that she is the Bride of Kong.

Of course King Kong comes to claim her, but instead of killing her, he falls in love with her. As he is carrying her back to his cave, he must defend her from various prehistoric creatures such as a Tyrannosaurus rex and a Pterodactyl. In the meantime, a crew of sailors, led by Fay's sweetheart, the mate from the ship, give chase.

Fay Wray screams while Kong fights off a pterodactyl in King Kong *(RKO, 1933).*

Originally, there was a scene in *King Kong* in which the giant ape, finding the pursuing sailors trying to cross a chasm by means of a log that has fallen across the abyss, picks up the log and throws it down to the bottom. Then along comes a giant spider who proceeds to consume these nautical Miss Muffets. For some reason the authors of the film thought that the spider scene was too grisly and cut it from the final print. The only thing remaining was the sailors falling through the air and bouncing on the bottom of the chasm.

Finally, the desperate hero finds Fay, brings her back to the village, and prepares to fight off King Kong, who is following. Denham is able to use gas bombs on Kong, bring him back to New York, and exhibit him in a theater.

As newspaper photographers are taking pictures of Fay, Kong thinks that the flashbulbs are doing harm to her. He breaks free from his chains and escapes.

He finds Fay in her hotel room, reaches in through an open window, grabs her, and carries her to the top of the Empire State Building. The air force is called out, and airmen fly around Kong, shooting him with hundreds of bullets. The gorilla, mortally wounded, tenderly lays Fay down in a safe place, and falls to the street below—stone dead. Denham confides to a passing policeman, "It was beauty killed the beast."

One thing that *King Kong* had going for it was suspense. Most of the subsequent giant monster films made the mistake of hitting us in the eye with a view of the monster right away. The delicious buildup of terror in *King Kong,* in which no unusual animal appears for the first half hour of the picture, has basically been lost.

Schoedsack, O'Brien, and Armstrong came back the same year with an atrocity called *Son of Kong.* Denham goes back to the island and finds a huge white gorilla—allegedly the son of Kong, but who his mother could have been was never explained. Kong's son is a gentle animal, befriending Denham when the producer bandages the ape's sore finger.

At the end of the film, the island is sinking and the poor gorilla is holding Denham in his upraised hand as the water gradually rises over his head. Denham is rescued by a boat, the island is no more, and gone is the great white gorilla.

The whole huge ape idea returned in 1949, with the release of *Mighty Joe Young.* O'Brien won an Academy Award for his special effects for this one.

Joe Young is a ten-foot-high gorilla who is the household pet of a sweet little orphan girl who is being raised in Africa. A man arrives and persuades the girl and her pet to go to the United States and show off.

Joe and the girl end up in a night club where Joe holds up a grand piano while the girl plays "Beautiful Dreamer." Of course, a la *King Kong,* Joe thinks that all of those people are there to hurt his mistress, and he goes berserk.

He is forgiven when he is the hero of a fire in an orphanage, climbing up and rescuing the children. At the end, he and Miss Moore are back in Africa, presumably to live happily ever after.

Incidentally, the showmen in *King Kong* and *Mighty Joe Young* were both played by the same man—Robert Armstrong.

It would seem that, starting with Kong, most of these huge creatures end up in horrible battles on the streets of some big city or other. Why they didn't stay in the country is hard to figure out. Kong, of course, had no choice, but how do you explain all of those other creatures wandering into London, Tokyo, Washington, San Francisco, and New York?

In 1951, *The Thing* arrived. A ship from outer space crashes somewhere in the Arctic. The driver is a horrible man-vegetable some eight feet in height, played by James

Arness long before he caught on as Matt Dillon in *Gunsmoke*. Naturally, there is a group of army research people nearby, and they haul this thing into their shelter, since he is now frozen in a block of ice.

Unfortunately the "thing" thaws out and starts prowling around the barren countryside. He might have been some distant relative of Dracula, since he dines off blood. In the meantime, one of the sled dogs has bitten off his hand. It turns out that the monster can grow a new hand, and from under the fingernails of the missing hand appear seeds that can possibly grow new thing-monsters.

The thing cannot be killed by bullets and it is thriving in the cold climate. The solution is that the group of humans fries the monster in an electric trap.

In the same year, along came *The Man from Planet X,* who was supposed to get the natives of a Scottish village to join forces with the invaders from his planet. This was the forerunner of *It Came from Outer Space* (1953), *The Invaders from Mars* (1953), *The Phantom from Space* (1953), *Killers from Space* (1954), *The Monolith Monsters* (1957), and *The Blob* (1958).

There is a small clique of monster movie fans who think that the last named film was one of the best. Perhaps it was a fine performance by Steve McQueen, then quite young, that set it apart. Or perhaps it is the small-town atmosphere of the picture that makes it more scary. We can believe that monsters go to the city more readily than we will accept the creature who attacked a small town.

The blob has killed the country doctor and goes right

on growing. Several victims later, he is huge, looking like a sort of giant wad of bubble gum. In the end he completely envelops a small diner in which McQueen and a few others are trapped. The blob is finally knocked out by being frozen (this was McQueen's idea) and is then dropped onto the ice of the polar seas where he cannot thaw out and return to civilization—or can he?

There have been lots more. In the 1953 production of *The War of the Worlds*, H. G. Wells's thriller, the real stars were armored intelligent creatures who came from Mars in order to conquer the earth. But the visitors were laid low by a simple epidemic of the common cold.

The Beast from 20,000 Fathoms was a dinosaur awakened from his sleep in 1953 by atomic testing.

In a film of 1954, *The Creature from the Black Lagoon* arrived. Producer Jack Arnold had borrowed the swamp idea from some Frankenstein and mummy movies and had his monster rise up out of the mud. The poor thing came back in 1955 in *The Revenge of the Creature.*

In both of these productions, the creature is portrayed as a jealous madman, and the girl who is the heroine never seems to wear anything but a bathing suit.

In John Sherwood's third of this series, a small change was made. In *The Creature Walks Among Us,* the monster has an unhappy love affair and thus finds out about the pain of unrequited love. He is a scaly monster, with what look like gills around his ears, long webbed fingers and toes, and a fish face. Oddly enough, although he spent most of his life at the bottom of the lagoon, when he

Ricou Browning, as
The Creature from
the Black Lagoon,
boards a boat
(Universal, 1954).

comes to the surface he never seems to have any mud or water plants on his body.

In *Them* (1954), another atomic explosion causes the ants of New Mexico to increase their size at least a hundredfold. The next year saw a giant spider in *Tarantula*.

Not to be outdone, the Japanese company, Toho, produced *Godzilla, King of the Monsters* in 1955. This creature looks a lot like a fat Tyrranosaurus, except he has a long tail and plates that stick up along his spine.

Godzilla has atomic breath, the better to destroy whole cities. That is, when he is not merely mashing them

Godzilla *is about ready to use his atomic breath (Toho, 1955).*

with his feet. This monster comes up from the depths of the sea in order to destroy Tokyo and is finally eliminated by atomic energy.

No, that's a lie. He had to be put back together for *The Return of Godzilla, Godzilla Versus the Thing, Son of Godzilla,* and *King Kong Versus Godzilla.* The reason was that Godzilla was the hottest property that Toho Studios had at the time. But in 1962 they came back with another friendly monster called *Mothra,* who was—you guessed it —a giant moth. Let's not go into either *Mothra* or its sequels, except to say that it eventually met Godzilla and won.

Then there was *It Came from Beneath the Sea* in 1955. The creature here was a giant octopus.

In 1957, even a praying mantis was made to grow to heroic proportions. The movie was called *The Deadly Mantis.*

130

EPILOGUE

Monster movies have come a long way from Méliès's first attempts in 1896. Great stars emerged, such as Lon Chaney, Sr., followed by Boris Karloff and Bela Lugosi. Now, Peter Cushing, Christopher Lee, and Vincent Price seem to have assumed their mantles. Cushing plays the suave, no-nonsense type of mad scientist, whose sense of authority and competency never waver. Lee is great as the vampire, the Frankenstein monster, and the mummy. Price can be the debonair crime investigator, the fiendish scientist, and the crippled monster, and make it look easy. And he seems to do it with a sense of humor.

Perhaps the film makers have come up with all of the

different types of monsters possible. But there is one kind of monster that may become the favorite of the future. It cannot be killed. It cannot be outwitted. It can only be unplugged.

Stanley Kubrick introduced us to this monster in his 1968 film, *2001: A Space Odyssey.* On the surface, this may have appeared to be a science fiction movie, but it was a true monster picture, and the name of the monster was Hal.

The scene is aboard a space ship, perhaps on its way to another galaxy. A computer named Hal plans all of the activities of the crew, whether they are awake or sleeping.

The problem is that the computer has a mind of its own. Instead of looking out for the welfare of the crew and doing their bidding, it rebels and sets out to do away with its masters. What is this but the man-made monster of the horror films?

The computer is the golem or the Frankenstein monster, projected into the future. It is more sophisticated than earlier monsters, and that makes it more dangerous. Indeed, it can outthink its own creators. It is able to be emotional at the point when it is finally, after the astronauts have discovered its plan, unplugged. It even suffers from electrical deprivation.

What will they think up next?

APPENDIX: MORE ABOUT SOME OF THE FILMS

A

ABBOTT AND COSTELLO MEET DR. JEKYLL AND MR. HYDE (Universal, 1953). *Director:* Charles Lamont. *With* Bud Abbott, Lou Costello, Boris Karloff, Craig Stevens.

ABBOTT AND COSTELLO MEET FRANKENSTEIN (Universal, 1948). *Director:* Charles Barton. *With* Bud Abbott, Lou Costello, Lon Chaney, Jr., Bela Lugosi, Glenn Strange.

ABBOTT AND COSTELLO MEET THE MUMMY (Universal, 1954). *Director:* Charles Lamont. *With* Bud Abbott, Lou Costello, Edwin Parker.

ANDERER, DER (Vitaskop, 1913). *Director:* Max Mack. *With* Albert Basserman.

AZTEC MUMMY, THE (Calderon, 1960). *Director:* King Miller. *With* Ramon Gay, Steve Grant.

B

BEAST FROM 20,000 FATHOMS, THE (Warner Brothers, 1953). *Director:* Eugene Lourie. *With* Paul Christian, Paula Raymond, Cecil Kellaway, Lee Van Cleef.

BEAST OF HOLLOW MOUNTAIN, THE (United Artists, 1956). *Director:* Edward Nassour, Ismael Rodriguez. *With* Guy Madison, Patricia Medina.

BEAST OF YUCCA FLATS, THE (Cardoza, 1961). *Director:* Coleman Francis. *With* Tor Johnson, Barbara Francis.

BELLS, THE (Chadwick, 1926). *Director:* James Young. *With* Lionel Barrymore, Boris Karloff.

BILLY THE KID VERSUS DRACULA (Circle, 1965). *Director:* William Beaudine. *With* John Carradine.

BLACK SABBATH (Emmepi-Galatea, 1963). *Director:* Mario Bava. *With* Boris Karloff, Susy Andersen.

BLACK SUNDAY (Galatea-Jolly, 1960). *Director:* Mario Bava. *With* Barbara Steele, John Richardson.

BLOB, THE (Paramount, 1958). *Director:* Irvin S. Yeaworth, Jr. *With* Steve McQueen, Aneta Corseaut.

BLOOD OF DRACULA (American International, 1957).

Director: Herbert L. Strock. *With* Sandra Harrison, Louise Lewis, Heather Ames.

BLOOD OF THE VAMPIRE (Tempean, 1958). *Director:* Henry Cass. *With* Donald Wolfit, Barbara Shelley.

BLOODY VAMPIRE, THE (Mexico, 1961). *Director:* Miguel Morayta. *With* Carlos Agosti.

BOWERY AT MIDNIGHT (Monogram, 1942). *Director:* Wallace Fox. *With* Bela Lugosi, John Archer.

BRIDE OF FRANKENSTEIN, THE (Universal, 1935). *Director:* James Whale. *With* Boris Karloff, Colin Clive, Elsa Lanchester, Ernest Thesiger, Dwight Frye, Una O'Conner, Mary Gordon, Walter Brennan, John Carradine.

BRIDES OF DRACULA (Hammer, 1960). *Director:* Terence Fisher. *With* Peter Cushing, Martita Hunt, Yvonne Monlaur.

BRING ME THE VAMPIRE (Mexico, 1965). *Director:* Charles Riquelme. *With* Mary St. Martin.

C

CABINET OF DR. CALIGARI, THE (Decla-Bioscop, 1920). *Director:* Robert Wiene. *With* Werner Krauss, Conrad Veidt, Lil Dagover.

CALTIKI, THE IMMORTAL MONSTER (Galatea Film/Bruno Vailati, 1959). *Director:* Robert Hampton (Riccardo Freda). *With* John Merivale, Didi Perego.

CAPTIVE WILD WOMAN (Universal, 1943). *Director:* Edward Dmytryk. *With* Aquanetta, John Carradine,

Evelyn Ankers, Milburn Stone, Martha Vickers, Paul Fix.

CONQUEST OF THE POLE, THE (Star Films, 1912). *Director:* Georges Méliès.

CREATURE FROM THE BLACK LAGOON, THE (Universal, 1954). *Director:* Jack Arnold. *With* Richard Carlson, Julia Adams, Richard Denning, Ricou Browning, Whit Bissell.

CRY OF THE WEREWOLF, THE (Columbia, 1944). *Director:* Henry Levin. *With* Nina Foch, Stephen Crane, Osa Massen.

CURSE OF FRANKENSTEIN, THE (Hammer, 1957). *Director:* Terence Fisher. *With* Peter Cushing, Christopher Lee, Hazel Court.

CURSE OF THE FLY, THE (Lippert, 1965). *Director:* Don Sharp. *With* Brian Donlevy, Carole Gray.

CURSE OF THE MUMMY'S TOMB, THE (Hammer-Swallow, 1964). *Director:* Michael Carreras. *With* Ronald Howard, Terence Morgan, Fred Clark.

CURSE OF THE WEREWOLF, THE (Hammer, 1961). *Director:* Terence Fisher. *With* Oliver Reed, Clifford Evans, Yvonne Romain.

D

DAUGHTER OF DR. JEKYLL (Allied Artists, 1957). *Director:* Edgar G. Ulmer. *With* Gloria Talbott, John Agar.

DEAD MEN WALK (Producers' Releasing Corporation, 1943). *Director:* Sam Newfield. *With* George Zucco, Mary Carlisle, Dwight Frye.

DEADLY MANTIS, THE (Universal, 1957). *Director:* Nathan Juran. *With* Craig Stevens, William Hopper.

DEVIL BAT, THE (Producers' Releasing Corporation, 1940). *Director:* Jean Yarbrough. *With* Bela Lugosi, Dave O'Brien.

DEVIL BAT'S DAUGHTER (Producers' Releasing Corporation, 1946). *Director:* Frank Wisbar. *With* Rosemary La Planch.

DEVIL'S CASTLE, THE (Robert-Houdin, 1896). *Director:* Georges Méliès.

DINOSAUR AND THE MISSING LINK, THE (Edison Company, 1917). *Director:* Willis H. O'Brien.

DOCTOR BLOOD'S COFFIN (Caralan, 1960). *Director:* Sidney J. Furie. *With* Kieron Moore, Hazel Court, Ian Hunter.

DR. CYCLOPS (Paramount, 1940). *Director:* Ernest B. Schoedsack. *With* Albert Dekker, Janice Logan.

DR. JEKYLL AND MR. HYDE (Selig Polyscope, 1908).

DR. JEKYLL AND MR. HYDE (Nordisk, 1910). *Director:* August Blom. *With* Alwin Neuss.

DR. JEKYLL AND MR. HYDE (Thanhauser, 1912). *Director:* Lucius Henderson. *With* James Cruze, Marguerite Snow, Harry Benham.

DR. JEKYLL AND MR. HYDE (Kineto-Kinemacolor, 1913).

DR. JEKYLL AND MR. HYDE (Imp, 1913). *Director:* King Baggott. *With* King Baggott, Jane Gail.

DR. JEKYLL AND MR. HYDE (Paramount, 1920). *Director:* John S. Robertson. *With* John Barrymore, Nita Naldi, Louis Wolheim.

DR. JEKYLL AND MR. HYDE (Pioneer, 1920). *With* Sheldon Lewis, Gladys Field.

DR. JEKYLL AND MR. HYDE (Paramount, 1932). *Director:* Rouben Mamoulian. *With* Fredric March, Miriam Hopkins, Rose Hobart.

DR. JEKYLL AND MR. HYDE (MGM, 1941). *Director:* Victor Fleming. *With* Spencer Tracy, Ingrid Bergman, Lana Turner, Ian Hunter, Donald Crisp, Barton MacLane, C. Aubrey Smith.

DOTTOR JEKYLL, IL (Sono, 1951). *Director:* Mario Scoffi. *With* Mario Scoffi, Anna Maria Campoy.

DRACULA (Universal, 1931). *Director:* Tod Browning. *With* Bela Lugosi, Helen Chandler, Dwight Frye.

DRACULA HAS RISEN FROM THE GRAVE (Hammer, 1968). *Director:* Freddie Francis. *With* Christopher Lee, Rupert Davies, Veronica Carlson.

DRACULA, PRINCE OF DARKNESS (Hammer, 1965). *Director:* Terence Fisher. *With* Christopher Lee, Barbara Shelley.

DRACULA'S DAUGHTER (Universal, 1936). *Director:* Lambert Hillyer. *With* Gloria Holden, Otto Kruger, Hedda Hopper.

DUST OF EGYPT, THE (Vitagraph, 1915). *Director:* George Baker. *With* Antonio Moreno, Edith Storey.

E

EMPEROR AND THE GOLEM, THE (State, 1951). *Director:* Martin Fric. *With* Jan Werich.

EVIL OF FRANKENSTEIN, THE (Hammer, 1964). *Director:* Freddie Francis. *With* Peter Cushing.

EYES OF THE MUMMY, THE (Union, 1918). *Director:* Ernst Lubitsch. *With* Pola Negri, Emil Jannings.

F

FEARLESS VAMPIRE KILLERS, THE (Cadre, 1967). *Director:* Roman Polanski. *With* Sharon Tate, Jack Mac-Gowran.

FLY, THE (Twentieth Century–Fox, 1958). *Director:* Kurt Neumann. *With* David Hedison, Patricia Owens, Vincent Price, Herbert Marshall.

FRANKENSTEIN (Edison, 1910). *Director:* J. Searle Dawley. *With* Charles Ogle.

FRANKENSTEIN (Universal, 1931). *Director:* James Whale. *With* Boris Karloff, Colin Clive, Mae Clark, John Boles, Dwight Frye.

FRANKENSTEIN CONQUERS THE WORLD (Toho, 1965). *Director:* Inoshiro Honda. *With* Nick Adams.

FRANKENSTEIN CREATED WOMAN (Hammer, 1967). *Director:* Terence Fisher. *With* Peter Cushing, Robert Morris.

FRANKENSTEIN'S DAUGHTER (Astor, 1958). *Director:* Richard Cunha. *With* Donald Murphy, Sandra Knight.

FRANKENSTEIN MEETS THE SPACE MONSTER (Vernon, 1965). *Director:* Robert Gaffney. *With* Robert Reilly.

FRANKENSTEIN MEETS THE WOLF MAN (Universal, 1943). *Director:* Roy William Neill. *With* Ilona Massey, Patrick Knowles, Lon Chaney, Jr., Lionel Atwill, Bela Lugosi, Maria Ouspenskaya, Dwight Frye.

FRANKENSTEIN MUST BE DESTROYED (Hammer, 1969). *Director:* Terence Fisher. *With* Peter Cushing.

FRANKENSTEIN 1970 (Allied Artists, 1958). *Director:* Howard W. Koch. *With* Boris Karloff, Tom Duggan.

G

GHOST BREAKERS, THE (Paramount, 1940). *Director:* George Marshall. *With* Bob Hope, Paulette Goddard, Richard Carlson, Anthony Quinn, Paul Lukas.

GHOST OF FRANKENSTEIN, THE (Universal, 1942). *Director:* Erle C. Kenton. *With* Sir Cedrick Hardwicke, Lon Chaney, Jr., Ralph Bellamy, Lionel Atwill, Bela Lugosi.

GIANT BEHEMOTH, THE (Artistes Alliance, 1959). *Director:* Douglas Hickox, Eugene Lourie. *With* Gene Evans.

GODZILLA, KING OF THE MONSTERS (Toho, 1955). *Director:* Inoshiro Honda. *With* Raymond Burr.

GOLEM, DER (Bioscop, 1915). *Director:* Paul Wegener,

Henrik Galeen. *With* Paul Wegener, Lyda Salmonova, Henrik Galeen.

GOLEM, DER (UFA, 1920). *Director:* Paul Wegener, Carl Boese. *With* Paul Wegener, Lyda Salmonova.

GOLEM, LE (Metropolis Pictures, 1936). *Director:* Julien Duvivier. *With* Harry Baur.

GOLEM, LE (ORTF, 1966). *Director:* Jean Kerchbron. *With* Andre Reybaz.

GOLEM UND DIE TÄNZERIN, DER (Bioscop, 1917). *Director:* Paul Wegener. *With* Paul Wegener, Lyda Salmonova.

GOLIATH AND THE VAMPIRES (Moffa, 1961). *Director:* Giacomo Gentilomo. *With* Gordon Scott, Gianna Maria Canale, Jacques Sernas.

H

HOMUNCULUS (Bioscop, 1916). *Director:* Otto Rippert. *With* Frederich Kuhn.

HORROR OF DRACULA (Hammer, 1958). *Director:* Terence Fisher. *With* Christopher Lee, Peter Cushing.

HOUSE OF DRACULA (Universal, 1945). *Director:* Erle C. Kenton. *with* Lon Chaney, Jr., Martha O'Driscoll, John Carradine, Lionel Atwill, Glenn Strange.

HOUSE OF FRANKENSTEIN (Universal, 1944). *Director:* Erle C. Kenton. *With* Boris Karloff, Lon Chaney, Jr., J. Carrol Naish, Elena Verdugo, John Carradine, Lionel Atwill, George Zucco, Glenn Strange.

HOUSE OF FRIGHT (Hammer, 1960). *Director:* Terence Fisher. *With* Paul Massie, Christopher Lee.

HOUSE OF WAX (Warner Brothers, 1953). *Director:* Andre deToth. *With* Vincent Price, Phyllis Kirk, Carolyn Jones, Charles Bronson.

I

I WALKED WITH A ZOMBIE (RKO, 1943). *Director:* Jacques Tourneur. *With* James Ellison, Francis Dee, Tom Conway.

I WAS A TEENAGE FRANKENSTEIN (American International, 1957). *Director:* Herbert L. Strock. *With* Whit Bissell, Phyllis Coates, Gary Conway.

I WAS A TEENAGE WEREWOLF (American International, 1957). *Director:* Gene Fowler, Jr. *With* Michael Landon, Whit Bissell, Guy Williams.

THE INCREDIBLY STRANGE CREATURES WHO STOPPED LIVING AND BECAME MIXED-UP ZOMBIES (Hollywood Star, 1965). *Director:* Ray Steckler. *With* Cash Flagg, Brett O'Hara.

INVADERS FROM MARS (Twentieth Century-Fox, 1953). *Director:* William Cameron Menzies. *With* Helena Carter, Arthur Franz, Leif Erickson, Hillary Brooke.

INVASION OF THE BODY SNATCHERS (Allied Artists, 1956). *Director:* Don Siegel. *With* Kevin McCarthy, Dana Wynter, Carolyn Jones, King Donovan, Larry Gates.

INVASION OF THE VAMPIRES (Mexico, 1962). *Director:* Alfonso C. Blake. *With* Erna Martha Bauman.
INVISIBLE MAN, THE (Universal, 1933). *Director:* James Whale. *With* Claude Rains, Gloria Stuart.
INVISIBLE MAN RETURNS, THE (Universal, 1940). *Director:* Joe May. *With* Sir Cedric Hardwicke, Vincent Price, Alan Napier.
ISLAND OF LOST SOULS (Paramount, 1933). *Director:* Erle C. Kenton. *With* Charles Laughton, Bela Lugosi, Richard Arlen, Leila Hyams.
IT (Goldstar, 1966). *Director:* Herbert J. Leder. *With* Roddy McDowall, Jill Haworth.
IT CAME FROM BENEATH THE SEA (Columbia, 1955). *Director:* Robert Gordon. *With* Kenneth Tobey.
IT CAME FROM OUTER SPACE (Universal, 1953). *Director:* Jack Arnold. *With* Richard Carlson, Barbara Rush.

J

JANUSKOPF, DER (Lippow/Decla-Bioscop, 1920). *Director:* F. W. Murnau. *With* Conrad Veidt.
JESSE JAMES MEETS FRANKENSTEIN'S DAUGHTER (Circle, 1965). *Director:* William Beaudine *With* Narda Onyx, John Lupton.
JUNGLE CAPTIVE (Universal, 1945). *Director:* Harold Young. *With* Otto Kruger, Vicky Lane.
JUNGLE WOMAN (Universal, 1944). *Director:* Reginald

LeBorg. *With* Evelyn Ankers, Aquanetta, J. Carrol Naish, Milburn Stone.

K

KILLERS FROM SPACE (RKO, 1954). *Director:* W. Lee Wilder. *With* Peter Graves.

KING KONG (RKO, 1933). *Director:* Merian C. Cooper, Ernest B. Schoedsack. *With* Fay Wray, Robert Armstrong, Bruce Cabot.

KING OF THE ZOMBIES (Monogram, 1941). *Director:* Jean Yarbrough. *With* Henry Victor, Dick Purcell.

KISS OF THE VAMPIRE (Hammer, 1962). *Director:* Don Sharp. *With* Noel Willman.

L

LIFE WITHOUT SOUL (Ocean Film Corporation, 1915). *Director:* Joseph W. Smiley. *With* Percy Darrell Standing.

LONDON AFTER MIDNIGHT (MGM, 1927). *Director:* Tod Browning. *With* Lon Chaney, Sr., Conrad Nagel.

LOST WORLD, THE (First National–Watterson R. Rothacker, 1925). *Director:* Harry Hoyt. *With* Bessie Love, Wallace Beery, Lewis Stone.

LOST WORLD, THE (Twentieth Century-Fox, 1960). *Director:* Irwin Allen. *With* Michael Rennie, Jill St. John, David Hedison, Claude Rains, Fernando Lamas.

LUST OF THE VAMPIRES (Titanus-Athena, 1957). *Director:* Riccardo Freda. *With* Gianna Maria Canale.

M

MAN FROM PLANET X, THE (United Artists–Wisberg-Pollexfen, 1951). *Director:* Edgar Ulmer. *With* Robert Clarke, William Schalert.

MAN-MADE MONSTER (Universal, 1941). *Director:* George Waggner. *With* Lionel Atwill, Lon Chaney, Jr., Anne Nagel.

MARK OF THE VAMPIRE (MGM, 1935). *Director:* Tod Browning. *With* Lionel Barrymore, Bela Lugosi, Lionel Atwill.

MIGHTY JOE YOUNG (RKO, 1949). *Director:* Ernest B. Schoedsack. *With* Terry Moore, Robert Armstrong.

MIO AMICO JEKYLL, IL (MG, 1960). *Director:* Marino Girolami. *With* Ugo Tognazzi, Abbe Lane.

MONOLITH MONSTERS, THE (Universal, 1957). *Director:* John Sherwood. *With* Grant Williams, Lola Albright.

MONSTER THAT CHALLENGED THE WORLD, THE (United Artists, 1957). *Director:* Arnold Laven. *With* Tim Holt, Hans Conried.

MOST DANGEROUS MAN ALIVE, THE (Columbia, 1961). *Director:* Allan Dwan. *With* Ron Randall, Debra Paget.

MOTHRA (Toho, 1962). *Director:* Inoshiro Honda. *With* Franky Sakai.

MUMMY, THE (Universal, 1932). *Director:* Karl Freund. *With* Boris Karloff, Zita Johann, David Manners, Bramwell Fletcher.

MUMMY, THE (Hammer, 1959). *Director:* Terence Fisher. *With* Peter Cushing, Christopher Lee.

MUMMY OF THE KING OF RAMSEE, THE (Lux, 1909). *Director:* Gerard Bourgeois.

MUMMY'S CURSE, THE (Universal, 1944). *Director:* Leslie Goodwins. *With* Lon Chaney, Jr., Martin Kosleck.

MUMMY'S GHOST, THE (Universal, 1944). *Director:* Reginald LeBorg. *With* John Carradine, Lon Chaney, Jr., Barton MacLane, George Zucco.

MUMMY'S HAND, THE (Universal, 1940). *Director:* Christy Cabanne. *With* Tom Tyler, Dick Foran, George Zucco.

MUMMY'S SHROUD, THE (Hammer, 1967). *Director:* John Gilling. *With* Andre Morell.

MUMMY'S TOMB, THE (Universal, 1942). *Director:* Harold Young. *With* Lon Chaney, Jr., Dick Foran, George Zucco, Turhan Bey.

MY SON THE VAMPIRE (Renown, 1952). *Director:* John Gilling. *With* Bela Lugosi, Arthur Lucan.

MYSTERIOUS ISLAND (MGM, 1929). *Director:* Lucien Hubbard. *With* Lionel Barrymore.

MYSTERY OF THE WAX MUSEUM (Warner Brothers, 1933). *Director:* Michael Curtiz. *With* Lionel Atwill, Fay Wray.

N

NOSFERATU (Prana, 1922). *Director:* F. W. Murnau. *With* Max Schreck.

O

ORLACS HAENDE (Pan-film, 1925). *Director:* Robert Wiene. *With* Conrad Veidt.

P

PHANTOM FROM SPACE (United Artists, 1953). *Director:* W. Lee Wilder. *With* Ted Cooper.

PICTURE OF DORIAN GRAY, THE (MGM, 1945). *Director:* Albert Lewin. *With* George Sanders, Hurd Hatfield, Donna Reed, Angela Lansbury, Peter Lawford.

PLAGUE OF THE ZOMBIES (Hammer, 1966). *Director:* John Gilling. *With* Andre Morell.

PLAN 9 FROM OUTER SPACE (Reynolds, 1958). *Director:* Edward D. Wood, Jr. *With* Tor Johnson, Bela Lugosi, Vampira.

PLANET OF THE VAMPIRES (American International, 1965). *Director:* Mario Bava. *With* Barry Sullivan.

PLAYGIRLS AND THE VAMPIRE (Nord, 1960). *Director:* Piero Regnoli. *With* Walter Brandi.

PSYCHO (Paramount, 1960). *Director:* Alfred Hitchcock. *With* Anthony Perkins, Janet Leigh, Vera Miles, Martin Balsam.

R

RAVEN, THE (Universal, 1935). *Director:* Louis Friedlander. *With* Boris Karloff, Bela Lugosi.

RETURN OF THE FLY (Twentieth Century-Fox, 1959). *Director:* Edward Bernds. *With* Vincent Price, Brett Halsey.

RETURN OF THE VAMPIRE, THE (Columbia, 1944). *Director:* Lew Landers. *With* Bela Lugosi, Nina Foch.

REVENGE OF FRANKENSTEIN, THE (Hammer, 1958). *Director:* Terence Fisher. *With* Peter Cushing.

REVOLT OF THE ZOMBIES (Halperin, 1936). *Director:* Victor Halperin. *With* Dorothy Stone, Dean Jagger.

ROBOT VERSUS THE AZTEC MUMMY, THE (Calderon, 1962). *Director:* Rafael Portillo. *With* Ramon Gay.

S

SAMSON AND THE VAMPIRE WOMAN (TCRM, 1962). *Director:* Alfonso Corona Blake. *With* Lorena Velasquez.

SHE-WOLF OF LONDON (Universal, 1946). *Director:* Jean Yarbrough. *With* June Lockhart, Sara Hayden.

SLAUGHTER OF THE VAMPIRES (Mercur, 1962). *Director:* Roberto Mauri. *With* Walter Brandi.

SON OF DR. JEKYLL (Columbia, 1951). *Director:* Seymour Friedman. *With* Louis Hayward, Alexander Knox.

SON OF DRACULA (Universal, 1943). *Director:* Robert Siodmak. *With* Lon Chaney, Jr., Robert Paige, Evelyn Ankers, Louise Albritton.

SON OF FRANKENSTEIN (Universal, 1939). *Director:* Rowland V. Lee. *With* Basil Rathbone, Boris Karloff, Bela Lugosi, Lionel Atwill.

SON OF KONG (RKO, 1933). *Director:* Ernest B. Schoedsack. *With* Robert Armstrong, Helen Mack.

SPLIT, THE (Breakston, 1959). *Director:* George Breakston. *With* Peter Dyneley.

STUDENT OF PRAGUE, THE (Bioscop, 1913). *Director:* Stellan Rye. *With* Paul Wegener, Lyda Salmonova.

STUDENT OF PRAGUE, THE (Sokal, 1926). *Director:* Henrik Galeen. *With* Conrad Veidt, Werner Krauss.

T

TARANTULA (Universal, 1955). *Director:* Jack Arnold. *With* John Agar, Mara Corday, Leo G. Carroll.

TERROR CREATURES FROM THE GRAVE (MBS-GIA, 1965). *Director:* Massimo Pupillo. *With* Barbara Steele, Walter Brandi.

TESTAMENT OF DR. CORDELIER, THE (Jean Renoir–Sofirad, 1961). *Director:* Jean Renoir. *With* Jean-Louis Barrault.

TESTAMENTO DEL FRANKENSTEIN, EL (1964). *Director:* Jose Luis Madrid. *With* Gerard Landry.

THEM (Warner Brothers, 1954). *Director:* Gordon Douglas. *With* James Whitmore, Edmund Gwenn, James Arness.

THING, THE (RKO, 1951). *Director:* Howard Hawks. *With* Margaret Sheridan, Kenneth Tobey, James Arness.

TRAITE DU VAMPIRE, LA (France, 1960). *Director:* Pierre Boursons. *With* Jean Boullet.

TRIP TO THE MOON, A (Star, 1902). *Director:* Georges Méliès.

TUNNELING THE ENGLISH CHANNEL (Star, 1907). *Director:* Georges Méliès.

U

UNCLE WAS A VAMPIRE (Italy, 1962). *Director:* Pio Angeletti. *With* Christopher Lee.

UNDYING MONSTER, THE (Twentieth Century-Fox, 1942). *Director:* John Brahm. *With* James Ellison, Heather Angel.

V

VALLEY OF THE ZOMBIES (Republic, 1946). *Director:* Philip Ford. *With* Ian Keith.

VAMPIRE, THE (Kalem, 1913). *Director:* Robert Vignola. *With* Harry Millarde.

VAMPIRE AND THE BALLERINA, THE (UA, 1961). *Director:* Renato Polselli. *With* Walter Brandi.

VAMPIRE'S COFFIN, THE (ABSA, 1958). *Director:* Fernando Méndez. *With* Germán Robles.

VAMPIRE'S GHOST, THE (Republic, 1945). *Director:* Lesley Selander. *With* John Abbott, Grant Withers.
VAMPIRO, EL (Able Salazar/Cinematográfica ABSA, 1959). *Director:* Fernando Méndez. *With* Germán Robles.
VAMPIRO AECHECHA, EL (Mexico, 1962). *Director:* Nestor Zavade. *With* Blanca Del Prado.
VAMPIRO DELL'OPERA, IL (NIF, 1961). *Director:* Renato Polsilli. *With* Vittoria Prada.
VAMPYR (Les Films Carl Dreyer, 1932). *Director:* Carl Dreyer. *With* Julian West.
VILLAGE OF THE DAMNED, THE (MGM, 1960). *Director:* Wolf Rilla. *With* George Sanders, Barbara Shelley.
VOODOO ISLAND (Bel-Air, 1957). *Director:* Reginald LeBorg. *With* Boris Karloff.
VOODOO MAN, THE (Monogram, 1944). *Director:* William Beaudine. *With* Bela Lugosi, George Zucco, John Carradine.
VULTURE, THE (Homeric, 1966). *Director:* Lawrence Huntington. *With* Robert Hutton, Akim Tamiroff, Broderick Crawford.

W

WAR OF THE WORLDS, THE (Paramount, 1953). *Director:* Byron Haskin. *With* Gene Barry, Anne Robinson.

WAR OF THE ZOMBIES (Galatea, 1963). *Director:* Giuseppi Vari. *With* John Drew Barrymore.

WEREWOLF, THE (Bison, 1913). *Director:* Henry McRae.

WEREWOLF IN A GIRLS' DORMITORY (Royal, 1961). *Director:* Richard Benson. *With* Curt Lowens, Barbara Lass.

WEREWOLF OF LONDON, THE (Universal, 1935). *Director:* Stuart Walker. *With* Henry Hull, Warner Oland, Spring Byington.

WHITE ZOMBIE (Amusement Securities, 1932). *Director:* Victor Halperin. *With* Bela Lugosi, Madge Bellamy.

WOLF MAN, THE (Universal, 1941). *Director:* George Waggner. *With* Claude Rains, Ralph Bellamy, Warren William, Patrick Knowles, Bela Lugosi, Lon Chaney, Jr., Maria Ouspenskaya.

WRESTLING WOMEN VERSUS THE AZTEC MUMMY (Calderon, 1965). *Director:* Armand Sylvestre. *With* Lorena Velazquez.

Z

ZOMBIES OF MORA-TAU (Columbia, 1957). *Director:* Edward L. Kahn. *With* Gregg Palmer.

ZOMBIES ON BROADWAY (RKO, 1945). *Director:* Gordon Douglas. *With* Bela Lugosi, Wally Brown.

ACKNOWLEDGMENTS

Abel Salazar/Cinematográfica A.B.S.A., p. 104
American International Pictures, Inc., p. 66 (top)
Hammer Film Productions, p. 40, 66 (bottom), 105, 111
Paramount Pictures, p. 54, 56
RKO (copyrighted-RKO Radio Pictures, a division of RKO General, Inc.), p. 113, 124
Toho International, Inc., p. 130, 131
Courtesy of Twentieth Century-Fox, p. 67
United Artists Corporation, p. 16, 132
Universal Pictures, an MCA, Inc. Company, p. 31, 35, 61, 63, 81, 84, 99, 101, 107, 129

INDEX

ABOUT THE AUTHOR

Thomas G. Aylesworth was born in Valparaiso, Indiana, and received his A.B. and M.S. degrees from Indiana University and his Ph.D. from Ohio State University. He has been a high school teacher, a college professor and a senior editor of a junior high school weekly science newspaper, and is currently a senior editor at a major New York publishing house, as well as a writer of books for young readers on science, the occult, and movies. He lives in Stamford, Connecticut, with his wife, who is a teacher of art, and their two children.